Philippians

Hywel R Jones

Christian Focus Publications

Dedicated
to
the students of the London Theological Seminary

In general, the New International Version (NIV) has been used in this commentary. Where it is directly quoted, it appears in bold type. The New International Version is published by Hodder & Stoughton. Other versions referred to are the King James Version (KJV), and the New American Standard Bible (NASB).

© 1993 Hywel R Jones
ISBN 1 85792 046 5

published
by
Christian Focus Publications Ltd
Geanies House, Fearn, Ross-shire,
IV20 1TW, Scotland, Great Britain.

printed and bound in Great Britain
by
Cox & Wyman Ltd, Reading, Berkshire.

cover design
by
Donna Macleod

Contents

COMMENTARY

Dating of Paul's letters

There is not sufficient material in the New Testament to enable a firm chronology to be compiled of either the main events in Paul's life and ministry or his correspondence. However, using Acts as a historical source and trying to integrate the relevant material from the Epistles with that, something like the following outline seems to be acceptable.

Date	Event	Scripture Reference	Epistles
33-35	Conversion	Acts 9:1-17, Galatians 1:15,16	
35-37	Damascus, Arabia	Acts 9:19, Galatians 1:17	
37	First Jerusalem Visit	Galatians 1:18	
37-45	Tarsus and Cilicia	Acts 11:26	
45-47	Famine relief to Jerusalem	Acts 11:27-30	
46/7, 47/8	First Missionary Journey	Acts 13:1-14:26	
48-49	Council of Jerusalem	Acts 15	Galatians before (perhaps after) Council
48/9-51	Second Missionary Journey	Acts 15:36-18:21	1 & 2 Thessalonians
52-57	Third Missionary Journey	Acts 18:22-21:16	1& 2 Corinthians, Romans
57-62	From Caesarea to Rome	Acts 23:23-28:30	Ephesians, Philippians, Colossians, Philemon
62-68	Fourth Missionary Journey and Death		1 &2 Timothy, Titus

INTRODUCTION

A comparison of Paul's letter to the Philippians with the other New Testament letters which he had written just before it (1 and 2 Thessalonians; Galatians; 1 and 2 Corinthians and Romans) might seem to indicate that the church at Philippi had no censurable weaknesses whatsoever. Instinctively, we know that this cannot have been the case. Just as 'there is not a righteous man on earth who does what is right and never sins' (Ecclesiastes 7:20), so it is with churches. Though no doctrinal deviation or moral blemish is imputed to the church in this letter, a little investigation will uncover that some problems did exist. But more of that later. At this point, simply let it be noted that it was a church which could be prayed for (1:4), exhorted (1:27) and warned (3:1,2). Clearly, it did not have everything. It could gain more. It could even lose much of what it had. In those general but important respects, it was a church like every other, in any age and place. It could prosper; it could decline. The letter was written to enable it to grow (1:25).

Paul and Philippi

We have the historical account of how Paul came to Philippi in Acts 16:6-12. He had been directed there by what, even for him, were strange ways. He and his companions had first tried to enter the Roman province of Asia and then Bithynia in Mysia but were effectively hindered, not by foes of the gospel of Christ, but by the Spirit of Jesus himself. How this took place is not specified in the passage but a comparison with what is said in Acts 8:29,39 about Philip and the

Ethiopian eunuch may cast some light on the matter. In that account we have the Spirit addressing Philip and then constraining his rapid departure. What happened to Paul and his companions could have been similar.

In any case, Paul was led down to Troas, a seaport near the ancient city of Troy. There, with the Aegean Sea before him, he saw in a vision a man from Macedonia, appealing for help. That was the green light for which he had been waiting. In spite of the measure of blessing he had known in Troas (he had not been idle and had converts to leave there, cf. Acts 20:6,7) and though anxious about how Titus had been received by the church at Corinth (see 2 Corinthians 2:12,13), he sailed for Europe with Silas, Timothy and Luke in response to what they believed was the Lord's call. This was about 50 A.D. and Paul was on his second missionary journey. It would be useful to consult a map at this point.

An interesting suggestion has been made that the man whom Paul saw in the vision was none other than Luke. In support of this is the fact that Luke begins to figure in the story at precisely the point when Paul set sail for Philippi. Acts 16:10 uses the pronoun *we* which means that the author of the book of the Acts of the Apostles was with Paul, Timothy and Silas. If this identification of the man from Macedonia is not accepted, it is difficult to deduce from the text how Paul could have recognised the man in the vision as being from Macedonia. In addition, it seems that when Paul and his companions left Philippi Luke remained to care for the infant church. The evidence which points in this direction is that Acts 16:40 reads, 'Then *they* left' not *we*; and in Acts 20:5, which records Paul's return to Philippi, the *we* reappears. Could Luke have been from Philippi? It is perhaps no coincidence that there was a medical school there.

Macedonia and Philippi

Archaeological excavations which commenced at Philippi in
the early part of this century have continued and there is a
museum of fine artefacts at Kavalla, the modern Neapolis.
These confirm the picture which we have of the city from
Acts and Philippians. The ruins of the forum in which Paul
and Silas were brought before the authorities and sentenced
to imprisonment can be seen. A prison has also been found
in the city on whose remaining wall a plaque has been placed
with the inscription, *For me to live is Christ and to die is gain*.
Like Tarsus (Acts 21:39), Philippi was no ordinary city,
though it is now in ruins. It was a Roman colony and the
leading city of that part of Macedonia (Acts 16:12; Philippians 4:15).

Macedonia itself was a large tract of land in north eastern
Greece, rich in gold and very fertile as it swept down to the
sea. The city of Philippi was located to the south east of that
area with Neapolis as its seaport (Acts 16:11). It was so
named by its king, Philip 11, who captured it from the
Thasians around 300 B.C. Having enlarged and fortified it,
the city became the focal point of his kingdom. Soon an
empire existed under the rule of his well-known son, Alexander the Great, which stretched from the Aegean Sea in the
west to the River Indus in the east. Men from Philippi formed
the core of Alexander's army.

After his death, the empire of Alexander was divided
among his generals and each part began to decline. Rome
stepped in and seized Macedonia about 185 B.C., dividing it
into four parts in the interests of more effective administra-
tion. Philippi was included in the first of those regions and
though it was not the capital, (Amphipolis had that distinction, see Acts 17:1), it did not lose its former prestige. It was

the leading city of that part of Macedonia.

The next phase in the city's history was marked by its being granted the status of a colony. That came about as a result of the battle which took place there in 42 B.C. in which the armies of Mark Antony and Octavian defeated those of Brutus and Cassius, the assassins of Julius Caesar. Many of the war veterans were settled at Philippi. It is striking that the word for Philippians which Paul uses in 4:15 is Latin in its form and not Greek. Subsequently, the city's status was upgraded on two occasions. The first was after Octavian defeated Mark Antony at the battle of Actium in 31 B.C. and the second when he became emperor and took the name Augustus. The city then received its full honorific name which was *Colonia Augusta Iulia (Victrix) Philippiensis*, the name Iulia being included in recognition of Julius Caesar.

Having used their military might to conquer, invaders usually proceed to transform the new colony by giving prominence to their own language and culture, sometimes even imposing it with the force of law. Alexander the Great was renowned for this. By his efforts, an outlook on life which has become known as Hellenism was established throughout the empire and held its diverse peoples together. Greek became the *lingua franca* and its related philosophy, literature and science affected the culture of each member nation. This not only caused great problems for the Jews in Palestine in the period between the Old and New Testaments, but it also affected cities outside that region, for example, Philippi. Hellenism survived Alexander's death only to become overlaid with the Latin cultural ethos when his disintegrating kingdom was succeeded by the Roman military machine. So Philippi became a colony of the Roman empire.

In addition to its being a cockpit of history, Philippi was

strategically located from a geographical point of view. It stood at the junction where Rome and Greece in the west met Asia Minor to the east and it straddled the great military and trade route, the *Via Egnatia*, which ran between the Adriatic and the Aegean seas.

Monuments to the imperial cult existed side by side with sanctuaries for the gods of Egypt. Isis was regarded as the protector of Philippi from 42 B.C. and Serapis was recognised. Cybele, the great mother goddess, was also worshipped there. As Philippi was a cosmopolitan city, its religious outlook was syncretistic.

But what did its status as a colony amount to? It meant that it was not only a little bit of Italy beyond its borders, but even a miniature of Rome, the capital itself. It was under the *ius Italicum* (Italian law) which made its citizens exempt from poll and property taxes and gave them the right of self-government. They could not be flogged, nor could they be imprisoned except in very extreme cases. In addition, everyone had the right of appeal to the emperor. The cameo of life in Philippi which is presented in Acts 16 is true to fact. Naturally, Philippians were very conscious of the status of their city and their privileges as its citizens.

Paul and the Church at Philippi

The church did not have a very auspicious beginning in terms of its composition. But churches seldom do. Not many of the world's wise, rich or noble people will deign to believe the gospel (1 Corinthians 1:26). In Philippi, not enough Jewish men existed (were there any?) to form a synagogue, which Paul could have used as a launching pad for the gospel. He found out that a few women who espoused the Jewish religion met for prayer by a river (Gangites) outside the city and there, on the Sabbath, he began to speak about Jesus Christ. Lydia, a business woman who came from Thyatira, a town in southern Asia Minor, and who was not a native Jewess, believed the message and was baptized along with her household. The infant church met in her house (Acts 16:15).

According to Luke, the next stage in the preaching of the gospel at Philippi and the growth of the church there came about as a result of satanic opposition (Acts 16:16-22). A slave girl, whom Luke describes as being possessed with a spirit, *python*, and who was being taken advantage of by her owners, drew attention to them. The term *python* is derived from a Greek myth and refers to the snake or dragon which guarded the oracle at Delphi and was slain by Apollo. Perhaps she writhed like a python.

The description of this girl and the knowledge which she possessed of the real identity of Paul, his companions and the mission on which they were engaged is all of a piece with what we read of demon possession in the Gospels (Luke 4:34,41; 8:28). Demons know the truth (James 2:19) but have no love for it.

As well as disclosing information which was hidden from others, the girl could also have been a ventriloquist. These powers made her a valuable commodity to her owners. This whole incident relates to the realm of the demonic and, perhaps, its connection with idolatry (see 1 Corinthians 10:20).

This was a case of Satan trying to protect his kingdom (Luke 11:21, 22) and steal a march on the Christian cause. He was attempting to use the truth in the service of evil and to hinder the spread of the gospel by stirring up trouble for those who were seeking to make it known. While persecution and imprisonment did result for Paul and Silas as a result of the exorcism and the subsequent protest of the slave owners, it was to the cost and not the gain of the kingdom of Satan. Not only was the girl delivered, but the jailor and his household were saved through the message preached by Paul and Silas. What is more, the whole Christian cause was vindicated before the magistrates and in the eyes of the people, and the church was enlarged (Acts 16:23-40).

Paul and the Letter to the Philippians

Though Paul might have dictated this letter to Timothy who was with him, just as Tertius had been his amanuensis when he wrote the church at Rome (cf. Romans 16:22), the letter to the Philippians is no joint letter. Paul wrote (spoke) in the first person singular (cf. 1:3; 3:1). No reasonable query can be raised about its apostolic authorship. There are two questions, however, which must be considered with regard to this letter. The first concerns its literary unity and the second the location of its author.

Unity - Did Paul write this letter all at once?

There are those who think that the letter as we have it is a combination of two or three letters which Paul wrote to the Philippians at different times. In support of their view, they point to the following data in the letter itself:

(1). The use of the expression *Finally* in 3:1, the striking change of tone in 3:2, and the resumption of the call to rejoice in 4:4 isolate the intervening section. 3:2-21, then, is regarded as part of another letter which Paul wrote to the church.

(2). A similar argument and conclusion is presented in connection with 4:10-20 on the grounds of the use of the word *finally* in 4:8; the benediction in 4:20 and the different subject matter of 4:10-20.

A discussion of these verses and sections will be found at the relevant sections of the commentary but we content ourselves at this juncture with two points in reply to these theories. First, there is no extant manuscript of Philippians which lacks 3:2-21 and 4:10-20; and secondly it is harder to explain why anyone should insert these passages where they are than to find a reason why Paul put them there in the first place.

In addition, there is no hint, either in the letter or anywhere else in the New Testament, that Paul did write another letter to the Philippians. Even so, it is not possible to declare that he could not have done so. To recognise a possibility is one thing; to convert it into a fact and proceed on that basis to carve up the letter to the Philippians is quite another. To *write the same things* in 3:1 does not mean that he had written these things before. It means that he was now writing what he had previously spoken.

Location - Where was Paul imprisoned?

It is obvious that Paul was in prison when he wrote this letter (cf. 1:7,13,14; 2:17). Philippians comes from the same period as Ephesians, Colossians and Philemon which also indicate that they were written by Paul when he was in prison. 2 Timothy was also written from prison (cf. 2:9) but at a later time (See table). While the fact that Paul wrote Philippians as a prisoner is sure, the location of his imprisonment cannot be fixed with equal certainty.

Though Paul does not actually state in the letter where he was writing from, the determination of the place of his imprisonment is not completely a matter of guesswork. There are certain pointers in the text on this matter which have to be considered. In addition, they have to be harmonised with the record of Paul's movements which we have in the Acts of the Apostles. We will begin with the latter in presenting a sketch of this discussion and the conclusion adopted in this commentary.

Four imprisonments of Paul are recorded in the book of Acts. These were at Philippi (16:23); Jerusalem (21:33); Caesarea (23:35) and at Rome (28:16). Of these, Philippi obviously has to be discounted. The same applies to Jerusalem because Paul's imprisonment there was more in the nature of protective custody and, in any case, it was not long enough to allow for all the incidents which are mentioned in Philippians. As far as the evidence of Acts is concerned, the choice must therefore lie between Caesarea and Rome.

There are two references in Philippians which, at first sight, might seem to settle the matter in Rome's favour, namely, the references to the praetorium in 1:13 and to Caesar's household in 4:22. It has to be admitted, however, that these could apply to Caesarea on the basis that 'praetorium' is used of Herod's palace which was there (cf. Acts 23:35). But the noun *praetorion* was not only used to designate a place, namely, the tent in which the commander of an army resided; it also referred to people, namely, any detachment of guards which was stationed there.

The reference in 1:13, therefore, does not have to be to the members of the crack Praetorian guard who would have been at Rome. Further, the members of Caesar's household could refer to those who accompanied soldiers wherever they went. Other arguments have been presented in support of Caesarea as the place of origin but, as they depend on the validity of other unproven considerations for their force, we need not go into them here.

There is one point, however, which weighs heavily against

Caesarea as a place of origin for Philippians. It is that Paul, from what he wrote in that letter, seems to be awaiting the verdict of a court which he would have to regard as final (see 1:20; 2:17). It is not only difficult but even impossible to think of Paul deciding not to contest an unfavourable verdict from a lesser court, which Caesarea would be, having claimed his right to appeal to Caesar (Acts 25:11,12). For this reason alone, Caesarea can be set aside.

It seems, therefore, that the case for Rome as the place where Paul was imprisoned when he wrote Philippians is established. Extra support for a Roman origin is the fact that up until the eighteenth century, and even subsequently, the consensus of scholarly thinking from a wide range of theological perspectives did favour Rome. But there is another possible place of origin which has been proposed and some reference must be made to that theory. It relates to Ephesus.

While there is no record in Acts of Paul's having been imprisoned at Ephesus, it has to be admitted that he could have been. In the first place, Luke does not provide in that book a complete account of Paul's movements. Secondly, he was in Ephesus for a sufficient length of time for all that is recorded in Philippians to have taken place. Thirdly, when he wrote *been in prison more frequently* (2 Corinthians 11:23), he had, according to the Acts record, only been imprisoned once and that was at Philippi. It is therefore not totally impossible for him to have been imprisoned at Ephesus and ruins of a tower exist there which has been called Paul's prison.

Against an Ephesian imprisonment, however, is the general tone and overall impression which Luke gives in his narrative of Paul's time in Ephesus (cf. Acts 19), even though it is in summary form. The riot which took place there was concluded with a verdict from a legal assembly which did not involve imprisonment. The omission of any reference to an imprisonment having taken place in Ephesus tells against this theory as does also the fact that Paul would as surely have appealed to Caesar from Ephesus as from Caesarea in the event of its being necessary.

We adopt the view, therefore, that Rome is still the likeliest place from which Paul wrote this letter. Before drawing this discussion to a final conclusion, however, some notice ought to be taken of the main arguments which are brought against it by those who favour either Caesarea or Ephesus.

The first of these is that in Philippians 1:13, Paul very definitely refers to his being in chains. How can this relate to Acts 28:30,31 where it seems that Paul was merely under house arrest? A satisfactory answer to this consists of two strands. To begin with, it should be noted that these verses summarise only the first two years of his imprisonment which form the pre-trial period, and it is quite feasible that his circumstances could have altered for the worse after the trial. In addition, the references in Acts 28:16,20 to a guard and a chain ought not to be overlooked.

Secondly, it is argued that the number of communications and journeys between Paul and the Philippians which are referred to in the letter are, given the distance between Rome and Philippi which was about 1,200 miles, too many to fit in to the duration of Paul's imprisonment in Rome. This is the strongest argument against that location. The following is a list of the contacts between Paul and Philippi which seem to be required by the information which we have in the letter.

1. News of Paul's imprisonment had reached Philippi.

2. Epaphroditus had travelled from Philippi and handed over the gifts from the church (4:18).

3. News of his illness had reached Philippi.

4. Epaphroditus knew of the anxiety of the Philippians about him (2:26).

5. Paul was about to send Epaphroditus to Philippi with his letter (2:25,28).

6. Timothy would follow as soon as Paul had a clearer view about his own future (2:19-23).

7. Paul hoped to follow as soon as he was released (2:24).

The following observations are in order on this data. First, items 1-4 had already happened when Paul wrote the letter and they do not have to correspond to four journeys. The three journeys referred to in items 5-7 were to be undertaken in the near future. Consequently, the whole seven movements do not have to be fitted into the two years and a little more which was the duration of Paul's imprisonment in Rome (Acts 28).

The conclusion we draw, therefore, is that the traditional view of Rome being the place of origin for Philippians can stand. That is the position taken for the purpose of this commentary. The rock on which the other identifications both founder is the martyrdom atmosphere of chapter 1. By itself, this can be regarded as settling the question.

Why did Paul write?

Paul was not first and foremost a literary man. He was a preacher and a planter of churches, an apostle, not building on another's foundation (Romans 15:20). Even when in prison, he would not have turned to writing merely to while away the time.

Something constrained him to write and, from the actual

letter, a number of possibilities suggest themselves. First of all, there was a gift to be acknowledged which was a fresh, tangible reminder of the Philippians' loving concern for him (4:10ff.). Then, Paul realised that the Philippians were concerned about Epaphroditus' health (2:25-28). In addition, Paul's own welfare was a matter of concern to the Philippians. The apostle would have wanted to tell the church not only about himself, but also how the gospel was spreading even though he was in prison (1:12ff.). There can be no doubt but that all these facts entered into Paul's mind and would have been enough to lead him to write.

But if this were all, the result would have been a very personal letter between Paul and the church, of limited value and relevance to the church in every age and place. There is more in Philippians than information on these matters. If he were only writing for the reasons given, it is very doubtful whether he would have described either the mind of Christ (2:5ff.) or his own mind about Christ (3:7ff.).

What else, then, is there in the letter which may provide clues as to why Paul wrote? The answer, of course, relates to what he had heard about the church and its needs. Paul's writing was a substitute for his preaching ministry when, for one reason or another, he could not actually visit the church addressed. Though Philippians is conversational in tone, it is authoritative in character. Like Paul's other letters in the New Testament, it had a serious purpose, which was to edify (2 Corinthians 10:8).

What had Paul learned about the church? Two things are obvious in the letter. First of all, the church at Philippi was in some danger from its environment. This is referred to as early as 1:28,29 and then more fully in 3:2,18,19. It is because of this threat that there is so much autobiographical material

in the letter. Paul states and explains his reaction to these foes
to reinforce his instruction on this point to the Philippians.
The identity of these adversaries is discussed in the commentary when the actual verses in which they are referred to are
under consideration.

In addition to this, and making the threat more serious, was
the weakness of the church herself. There was a lack of unity
in the church and perhaps there was a perfectionist influence
creeping into it as well (3:13-15). Whether the latter is true
or not, there was a definite need for a unity which was deep
and wide. There are many appeals in the letter which indicate
this, for example, 1:27b; 2:1-4,14,15; 3:15-17. In addition,
the words *all of you* occur too often for them not to have been
deliberately chosen (cf. 1:4,7,8,25; 2:17,26). It might even be
that this lack of oneness in the church was traceable to the
alienation which had developed between two notable Christian women in the congregation, namely Euodia and Syntyche
(4:2). There is no need to accept the notion that the Lydia of
Acts 16 was so called because of the area she came from and
that her real name was either Euodia or Syntyche.

These needs of the church were, we believe, uppermost in
Paul's mind as he set himself to write the letter. But they
related to a greater concern. It was Paul's supreme concern
that the church at Philippi should continue to be a beacon for
the gospel. He saw the reality of opposition from without,
coupled with an air of spiritual unreality and lack of unity
within, as presenting an alarming threat to the progress of the
gospel.

The church had been in partnership with Paul in the
defence and confirmation of the gospel. That is what had
bound them together as one. Paul fervently desired this
practice to continue whether he was spared or not. He wrote,

therefore, that the church might be, and remain, truly evangelical, that is thoroughly characterised by the gospel.

All Paul's epistles are gospel-centred but in this one which is relatively brief, he refers to the gospel frequently, both by name and in terms of the appropriate experience of it (1:5,7,12,16,27; 2:22; 3:7ff.; 4:3,15). His concern is for a unity which becomes the gospel and, therefore, will advance it.

This is the perspective from which this commentary has been prepared. Paul is writing to a church of Christ (1:1) which has shown its genuine character by a concern for the spread of his gospel (1:5). However, it needs to live worthily of that gospel (1:27) and to do that, it must possess and express the mind of Christ (2:5). With the faith of the gospel, the mind of Christ and the supply of the Spirit (1:19), not only will believers make spiritual progress (1:25) but the gospel will too - in a crooked and depraved generation (2:15).

COMMENTARY

1. INTRODUCTION AND GREETING (1:1-2)

In the classical world of the first century, letters would normally begin with the name of the author, then the name of the person addressed and finally a greeting. Paul uses that literary convention here, as he does elsewhere, but fills it out with sacred truth. This is a particularly good example of the character of the entire Bible in which God expresses his mind and heart, but does not use a heavenly language or style to do so. If he had, the result would have been an unbreakable code for his people. Divine revelation and human recording are not incompatible; infallibility and intelligibility are not like the proverbial oil and water. The Bible is the word of God in human words (2 Peter 1:20-21; 2 Timothy 3:16-17).

A comparison of these verses with the opening of Paul's letters to other churches in the New Testament reveals a striking omission. It relates to the word *apostle*. It is only in writing to the Philippians, the Thessalonians and Philemon that Paul does not designate himself as an apostle of Jesus Christ in the introduction. That contrast can be highlighted still further by calling to mind that 1 Thessalonians does contain a specific reference to his being an apostle (2:7) and, in 2 Thessalonians there are some very emphatic assertions of the authority which belongs to that office (3:4,6,14). The fact is that out of all his letters to churches, it is only to the church at Philippi that he does not refer to the nature of his ministry and does not invoke the authority inherent in it. He even does that in writing to Timothy and Titus - but not to Philemon, his one personal letter in the New Testament.

What does this difference indicate with respect to the church at Philippi? It says that it was neither a church like the one at Rome which needed to be informed by Paul that he was an apostle of Jesus Christ; nor was it like the church at Corinth which needed to be reminded of that fact because it was entertaining doubts and denials about it. The Philippian church recognised and respected him as a special representative of Jesus Christ, having being authorised and endowed by him personally. In writing to the church at Philippi, Paul knew that he could refer to himself and Timothy in the same breath (nowhere else does he do this) as **servants of Christ Jesus**.

The term *doulos* (servant) which Paul actually used means *slave*. He chose this word to express the view which he and Timothy shared, that they had no independence and rights of their own, but belonged to another. It was to Jesus Christ that they belonged because they had been purchased (redeemed) by him and enrolled in his service (called). In the letters which Paul wrote at this time he referred to himself as the prisoner of Jesus Christ (Ephesians 3:1; 4:1; Philemon 1,9). Perhaps something of the dignity and authority of the prophets as servants of Jehovah in the Old Testament (see Jeremiah 7:25 and elsewhere) is also included in this expression.

The church at Philippi was made up of **saints** with their office-bearers (verse 1) and that is how a church should be thought of. It had evidently developed since Paul's first visit but, unlike developments which take place in many churches after their foundation, the church at Philippi had remained true to its nature. There had been numerical increase, but all who belonged to it could still be addressed as saints.

Being designated *saints* did not only mark out the Philippian believers as the people of God in a corporate sense as was the case with the Old Testament community (cf. Exodus 19:5,6). In the New Testament, this term refers to a divine work in the heart and its effects. It is more, much more than an externally discernible status. In the hearts of those who are saints, an initial and ineradicable separation from the world, purification from sin and consecration to God has taken place (see 1 Corinthians 6:11; 2 Thessalonians 2:13,14), though they do need to be made more holy (cf. Philippians 1:9,10,25; 2:1-5;12-14 etc.). The church was made up of those who professed to have been separated from sin to God. Saints, therefore, are those who are quickened from spiritual death by virtue of being united to Jesus Christ through faith and are not those who are merely baptized while living, or canonised after dying.

The church at Philippi seems to been have fairly large when Paul wrote because it had two kinds of office bearers, namely **overseers** (that is, elders) and **deacons**. These are to be understood in terms of the developments in church organisation which are recorded in the book of Acts. Diaconal ministry was most probably what was inaugurated in the church at Jerusalem (Acts 6:1-6), though the term *deacon* is not actually used there. The primary task of the deacons was relief for the poor and needy (cf. 1 Timothy 3:8-13).

Overseers were elders and not hierarchical bishops as in the contemporary use of the term. This can be deduced from the fact that these terms are used of the same men in Acts 20:17,28. Clearly, a number of elders/overseers existed and functioned in the one church at Philippi (cf. Acts 14:23; 1 Timothy 3:1-7; Titus 1:5-9). They watched over the spiritual life of the congregation. This development was patterned after the Jewish custom, referred to in the Gospels (Matthew 27:1), which itself goes back to Old Testament times (Exodus 18:13-26).

The kind of greeting Paul uses in verse 2 (and in other letters) expresses not only Christian good wishes but also a divinely given assurance of the blessings specified. The pronoun *you* is in the plural and it is therefore believers in church fellowship who are greeted and, by implication, prayed for in this salutation.

The distinctively Christian aspect of these greetings, which distinguishes them from secular forms on the one hand and Hebrew/Jewish expressions on the other, lies first in the mention of grace before peace and then in associating as suppliers of these blessings, the Lord Jesus Christ with God, the Father. We will consider each of these in turn.

Christian blessings
In letters written according to the Graeco-Roman pattern, the salutation would be *chairein* which means *greetings*. Paul substituted the word *charis* for this which meant something very different though it sounded similar. *Charis* - (grace) - pointed to God's good will toward believers and not human good wishes.

Peace (*shalom*) was the regular Hebrew greeting. It related to a person's well-being in all its aspects, religious, physical and material, both as an individual and as a member of the family or community. The inclusion of the physical as well as the spiritual was in keeping with the Abrahamic and Sinaitic covenants which promised spiritual blessings but in a national, material package. In addition, there were certain moral conditions to be met in order that those material blessings could be enjoyed by the nation (Deuteronomy 28-30).

Grace describes the way in which God deals with sinners on the basis of what Jesus Christ accomplished in his life and death. It is related to the freeness of the new covenant and opposed to the method of trying to earn or in any way merit spiritual blessings by means of human works of any kind (cf. Romans 4:4,5a; 11:6). These verses declare that the blessings of salvation are not bestowed because they have been earned or can be demanded. They oppose grace and human merit quite explicitly and prohibits any merging of them in terms of the basis on which salvation is given. If salvation is by grace, then it is no longer by works; if it were, grace would no longer be grace.

While grace has an Old Testament equivalent, namely, *chesedh*, that is, *lovingkindness* (exemplified supremely in the life of Hosea), it is primarily a new covenant reality and gives priority to a person's spiritual-moral well-being in the sight of God. In putting grace before peace, therefore, the new covenant is being given preference to the old, as is proper for an apostle of Christ, and Christians are being taught to think of their spiritual-moral well-being more highly than of anything physical and material (cf. 3 John 2).

Peace is the fruit of grace. As peace with God has been obtained through faith in Jesus Christ (Romans 5:1), it is, first, peace with God, second, peace within, and third, peace between believers that is referred to here, all whatever the outward circumstances (cf. 1:21; 4:7,9,11). Grace and peace are used to indicate that all the Old Testament looked forward to has been actualised.

As the word *covenant* has been used a number of times already and in significant ways, the term ought to be explained. It refers to a relationship between parties which is binding on both but not negotiated between them. In Philippians, the parties which are in view are either God and Israel, or God and Christian believers.

God entered into a covenant with Israel at Mount Sinai and regulated her life as a nation, in its civic and religious aspects

by his laws (cf. Exodus 19:4-6). This covenant is called *old*
in Hebrews 8:13. It is also called the *first* covenant in that
passage not because it was literally the first which God made
(he had made a covenant with Abraham and his descendants
before the Sinaitic covenant, Exodus 2:24, Galatians 3:17),
but because it was the first covenant made with a redeemed
company of people rather than an individual. Though it had
originally been made with a people who had been delivered
from an evil bondage, it could not make them or their
descendants holy. God therefore announced a new covenant
which would remove sin. This second covenant made the first
old. This new covenant is related to the coming of Jesus
Christ, the promised Messiah (Hebrews 8:6-13) and it brings
the Christian church into being.

The Christian God

Having been brought up as a devout Jew, Paul was convinced
that there was only one God. This meant that he not only
rejected the idol worship of the nations at large with their
heathen notions about God, but also the blasphemy of Christian
Jews in what they claimed for Jesus of Nazareth. After becoming a Christian, his thinking about God underwent a change. He
still affirmed the non-reality of other gods (see 1 Corinthians
8:4-6) but, strikingly, he now spoke of Jesus in the same
breath as the God who was one. In this verse he is designated
Lord and associated with God who is described as **Father**.

Jesus as Lord

Kurios (Lord) was the word which was used for earthly
dignitaries in the secular world. The Greek speaking Jews
who translated the Old Testament into Greek (the Septu-
agint) before the coming of Christ, also used it to render

Jehovah. In using it here, Paul is obviously giving to Jesus an exalted position and status above all human rulers. But there is more. Jesus is put on the same plane as God by being spoken of together with him as a joint-supplier of grace and peace. This amounts to a recognition of the deity of Jesus.

Though the term *Father* was used of God in the Old Testament, it was only used with regard to his relationship with Israel as a community or with her king as an individual. In the first, corporate, sense what the term pointed to was God's kindly care of his covenant people (for example Psalms 68:5 or 103:13). In Jeremiah 31:9, God says, 'I am Israel's father' (cf. also Isaiah 63:16; 64:8). The individual use of the term (2 Samuel 7:14) is to be understood within the kind of relationship just described because the king was to care for the people in God's name.

These uses of the term *Father* in the Old Testament fall short of the New Testament's use of the term. This is the result of the revelation of God in Christ, his eternal, beloved Son and the gift of the Holy Spirit through him (Luke 11:2; Galatians 4:4-7) to all who believe. No Old Testament believer ever addressed God as 'My Father'. The term is therefore lit up with extra meaning in the New Testament because each individual believer can address God as Father. Each shares in his character because each has been regenerated by him (1 Peter 1:3; 2 Peter 1:4) and in his dignity because each has been adopted into his family (Romans 8:15b-17; Galatians 4:6-7).

2. PRAYER - THANKSGIVING AND INTERCESSION (1:3-11)

Following the greeting, Paul usually thanks God for the church to which he is writing. God is acknowledged as the one who has brought the church into being, endowed and sustained it. He is therefore the only one who can supply its needs. That is what we have here.

Thanksgiving (1:3-8)

Paul was not only grateful for the church at Philippi but joyful on account of it. Whenever he thought of it, his heart was gladdened and he gave thanks to God. That was by no means the case with all the other churches he wrote to. What therefore was distinctive about Philippi?

The answer to this question is in verse 5. The NIV's translation **partnership in the gospel** states Paul's thought clearly. What he meant by partnership was not sharing in the blessings which the gospel gives, but sharing in the service which the gospel deserves as a result of the blessings received through it. The church at Philippi was energetic in the cause of the gospel and, what is more, it had been so from the beginning of its history.

In particular, the church had stood with Paul as he stood for the gospel.

Defending and **confirming** are legal terms and refer to the trial in which Paul had given testimony. The church had supported him in prayer and also done its own work in clearing the gospel from the false charges of the world, demonstrating its truth and power by the character of their living. That was what filled the apostle's heart with joy. How wrong it would have been for him to feel otherwise (cf. verse 7). He was a servant of Jesus Christ (verse 8) and it was the gospel of Christ (verse 27).

But all this was true of the Philippian believers because of the good work which God had begun (verse 6) in their hearts and lives. What is the nature of this good work? Is it their activity on behalf of the gospel, or is it God's regenerating work in their hearts? While adopting the latter as being what Paul had in mind, we do not exclude all reference to the former. Indeed, there is a straightforward way of seeing the relationship between them. It is that their good work for the gospel was the result of God's good work in them.

There is a very close connection between the gospel and the new birth. While the Holy Spirit works secretly implanting spiritual life in the sinner's dead heart (John 3:8), it is by responding to the word of God that the quickened begin to express their new found life (1 Peter 1:23). Although an understanding and appreciation of the importance of the gospel is the motivational factor in their service on its behalf, it is the result of God's gracious activity in their hearts and lives.

Though serving the interests of the gospel is a proof of having been born again, it is not the full product of it. Each day spent in this way is one more indication of the reality of that first day (verse 5) in an experience of the grace of God. But even those subsequent days, however many, costly and useful as they might be, are not the full product of it either. They supply proofs of the work being sustained. The NIV translation **carry on to completion** brings out the sense of the word better than the simple *complete*. It includes those days but points to more. Ultimately, its full result awaits the last day - the day of Jesus Christ (verses 6b, 10b; cf. 3:20,21)). Although a believer's experience and possession of salvation is greatly increased at death (cf. 1:23), even that does not coincide with the fullness of salvation.

So the first day was when the Lord Jesus Christ came to Philippi by virtue of the proclamation of the gospel, bringing people out of a crooked and depraved generation, spiritual darkness and death (2:15). The last day will be when he comes visibly, gloriously and in power and makes his believing subjects completely like himself in character (1:10,11) and in body (3:21). In between they are to live worthily of the gospel.

Intercession (1:9-11)

Paul's petition for the church at Philippi indicates his awareness of its need and also his confidence that God would be willing and able to supply what was lacking. But it also expresses his desire that God would do so. Prayer for other Christians not only tests one's confidence in God but also one's love for fellow believers. Though he intends to exhort the believers by means of what he is going to write to them, he begins by praying to God for them. This is because, ultimately, all spiritual growth comes from above. Should anyone preach or witness to others or offer advice without praying for them?

The bottom line of his supplication for them relates to their need to have their love increased - a seemingly universal and perennial deficiency in Christian churches. But to be exact, his desire is that it might abound more and more. This is one of the many superlatives in Paul's letters, but perhaps one that is not as well known or as well used as others. It is not a euphoric overstatement but a sober declaration of what is possible from God through Jesus Christ. Love (*agape*) is a word which Christians made their own. It involves giving to others to the extent of laying down one's life. It is a love like God's own love in Jesus Christ for sinful mankind (John

3:16). John comes nearest to a definition of this love. He writes: 'This is how God showed his love among us: He sent his only-begotten Son into the world that we might live through him. This is love: not that we loved God, but that he loved us and sent his Son to be an atoning sacrifice for our sins (1 John 4:9,10).

Paul's prayer reaches to two levels. It goes down to the basement in relation to the Philippians' depth of need and to the top floor in terms of God's resources. First, he prays that their love may become more mentally discriminating (verses 9,10) and that in two complementary ways. **Knowledge** refers to the content of divine truth. **Depth of insight** relates to a kind of skill in seeing its relevance and expressing it in the complexities of life's situations. It is something comparable to the wisdom commended and described in the book of Proverbs, the epistle of James and, of course, 1 Corinthians 13. Clearly, even Christians who know something of true love need to be informed and guided as to what to think and how to behave in day to day relationships and circumstances. This was the basic need of the Philippians.

Through gaining more and more of this loving 'know how' with regard to living for God among human beings, it becomes possible for believers to differentiate not only between bad and good, but between the good and the best. In this way character is moulded. Time and again in the letter Paul stresses the importance of right thinking regarding decisions which have to be made in personal devotion and corporate service in the cause of Christ. The frequent use of two verbs in this letter is relevant here. The verbs are *phroneo* and *hegeomai*. They are not far apart in meaning. The first means to *think* or *estimate* and is found in 1:7; 2:2,5; 3:15,19; 4:2,10. The second means to *consider* or *govern* in the sense of exerting an influence. This occurs in 2:3,6; 2:25; 3:7,8. Another verb *logizomai* is used twice (in 3:13 and 4:8) and this also refers to mental activity, meaning to *conclude* or *ponder*.

Making choices does not only deal with problems, it forms attitudes. When the choices have been right, character and conduct result which are generally neither displeasing to God nor blameworthy before men. Righteous words and deeds abound consistently and are displayed as such (see 4:8,9 and the comment on those verses). This will redound to the honour of God when Jesus Christ returns and everything will be revealed and consummated.

3. PERSONAL REPORT AND RESOLVE (1:12-26)

It is impossible to conceive of a letter between friends which does not contain personal details and news. The section before us can, therefore, be viewed very naturally from this perspective. It contains news - but news with a difference, the kind that Christians would like now and again to read in our papers!

What it contains is neither fiction nor propaganda. It is neither fabricated nor dressed up in the interests of telling a good story and grabbing attention - not even with Christians in view as the readership. It is factual information about the progress of the gospel, in circumstances which were perplexing, adverse and uncertain. The word which is used for 'progress' in verse 12 (*prokope*) means to make headway in spite of obstacles. It was the term used to describe the very real activity of pioneering scouts sent on ahead of a following army.

The news Paul had to give concerned the past and the future. In relation to the past, it was an encouraging report (verses 12-18); with regard to the future, it was an expectant resolution (verses 19-26). And what of the present i.e. the actual situation as he was writing? Paul was jubilant in that as well. He was neither an escapist nor a romantic. He could rejoice whichever way he looked (verses 18b; 3:1; 4:4).

The Past-Encouraging Report (verses 12-18)

In this brief review, Paul has much more to say about the gospel than about himself. No doubt, the Philippians would have liked more information - just as we would - about the character and conditions of his imprisonment. However, Paul exercises a reserve on this point. He only spoke in detail about his sufferings on one occasion, to the church at Corinth, and that was due to the higher consideration of defending the validity of his own apostleship (2 Corinthians 11:21ff.).

In this letter he only refers generally to the things that have happened to him such as the fact that he had to wear chains. What he wants to talk about is the spread of the gospel and the glorifying of Christ (verses 18-26). He had discovered once more, but this time in the capital city itself, that though he was suffering even to the point of being chained like a criminal, God's word was not chained (2 Timothy 2:9).

So the gospel had advanced even though Paul had been imprisoned. In the cell, in the guardroom, in the palace and abroad in the city, Christ was being preached. That gladdened his heart and he knew that it would have the same effect on the Philippians. Circumstances that are so obviously discouraging can be turned around by God in his providential activity. How sad and serious it is if a church or a Christian does not count on this happening or fails to see it when it does. It has been the case in the history of the church that the burning of the Bible has only served to set its message aflame

in more hearts. The same has been true even with the
sufferings and deaths of the saints.

Paul uses the word *preach* frequently in this section and
describes it as to **speak the word of God**. Though he does not
actually use the term of himself and his activity, there can be
no doubt but that it can be applied to him. Prison would not
silence him. But there were others who disseminated the
word beside himself. It seems that some of these were highly
unlikely and irregular from the point of view of the church.
They were his guards (verse 13) who told their barrack room
companions about him and what they heard from him. In this
way members of Caesar's household were informed about
him and so the gospel spread. The same sort of thing
happened as a result of the planting of the gospel in Thessalonica (cf. 1 Thessalonians 1:9). Observers of the effects of
the gospel in the lives of people from Thessalonica, which
was also in Macedonia, relayed the news for the apostle. It
seems possible that people in Caesar's household were
converted through hearing gospel truth through people who
were not themselves converted people!

But there were others as well and it is of these that Paul
uses the word *preach*. These were Christian men, although
there *is* a place in gospel work for Christian women (see 4:3
and comment there). Paul calls them all **brothers in the Lord**
(verse 14). Clearly he regards them as being related to Jesus
Christ just as the Philippians were: that is, they too were
saints. They were all preaching about faith in Jesus Christ
alone for salvation. The church at Rome had been founded by
those who had been present at Jerusalem on the Day of
Pentecost and who had been enlightened and empowered by
the Spirit on that special occasion (Acts 2:10). This was some
fifteen years or so before Paul arrived there.

There was, however, a difference between these preachers which the apostle deemed it important to record. Care must be taken so that it is not misconstrued. It was neither a distinction between them in terms of whether they were all Christians or not, nor whether their messages were true to the gospel of Christ or not. They were all brothers and were all preaching Christ. It is therefore quite inaccurate and unjustifiable for Paul's response in verse 18 to be urged as the way in which Christians today should regard anything which goes by the name of preaching. It is inconceivable that Paul would have rejoiced on account of the speaking of those referred to in 3:2,18, or said with indifference *what does it matter?* (see verse 18)

The difference lay in the realm of motivation. Paul's steadfastness in adversity had strengthened the spiritual nerve of many who had taken their courage in both hands and spoken out fearlessly in the name of the Lord. Paul does not express the slightest note of disapproval in connection with that motive, unless by *most* he deliberately meant to imply that some were not so animated. Timidity before one's adversaries is reprehensible in a preacher.

But the real dividing line was over *love*. There were those who were filling the gap which Paul's imprisonment had created, out of love for him and even more for the gospel. They were motivated by goodwill and wanted by their efforts to encourage Paul in his sufferings. But there were others who wanted to fill the gap to gain some notice and praise for themselves. They intended to make his imprisonment more difficult, either by making him unhappy or rousing the authorities against him. Whether they succeeded in the latter, we are not told. But they completely failed in the former design and their unworthy motivation only affected them-

selves. It is not only courage that a preacher needs but love
- and love in the sense of being willing to co-operate with
others whom God may be using more.

If the conditions of his imprisonment were made more
harsh as a result of the preachers just referred to, then Paul's
response is all the more striking. But it is worth noting
anyway. It is neither stoical nor just magnanimous. It is truly
gracious in perception and spirit. Paul sees that whatever the
motive, Christ is being preached and that brings him joy.
Courage, love and joy are becoming adornments for a gospel
preacher and, for that matter, anyone who witnesses to the
gospel. If God can, in his amazing providence, use the
unconverted to spread the gospel, may he not use his servants
even though their motives are not what they ought to be?

The Future Expectant Resolve (verses 19-26)
Paul's rejoicing does not evaporate when his outlook moves
from the known past to the unknown future. Indeed, the
reverse is the case. He seems to become more jubilant, not
less (verses 18,19). What was responsible for this? The
explanation lies in the kind of divine activity which he had
known in the past, with all that it implied, and which had
enabled him to rejoice then. The provision of gracious aid
(verse 7) and amazing providence (verse 12), confounding all
the natural deductions which could have been drawn from
what befell him, led Paul to conclude that something of the
same order would surely happen in the future. God had turned
his captivity so that the gospel was let loose. Would he not
turn his adversity so that it would issue in his *salvation*?

Before going further, some comment must be made about
the word *salvation* (NIV footnote) being given preference
over the word **deliverance** which appears in verse 19. In the

NIV preface we are informed that such footnotes were regarded by the translators either as having equal validity, or, if not as accurate, not to be totally dismissed. Clearly, there was a lack of agreement among the translators with regard to the meaning of *soteria* in verse 19.

Now it might seem that there is not much difference in meaning between salvation and deliverance. Certainly, in many places in the New Testament they could do service for each other and that applies to the verse being considered. This being the case, why are they put forward as alternatives or even set up in opposition to each other? The answer to this question lies in the uncertainty of scholars and commentators over whether Paul was thinking primarily/exclusively of release from prison when he used this word. The favouring of *deliverance* as a translation is linked to the view that he was.

We are, however, adopting the word *salvation* because it seems quite clear to us that Paul was thinking of something much greater than just release, significant though that would be. He was thinking of a big step forward in the matter of his own salvation, even to the point of its consummation. He explains what he means by salvation (verses 19,20) before he even alludes to release from prison and describes it as magnifying Christ in his body. His thought has moved from the advance of the gospel which he serves (verses 12ff.), to an advance in the salvation it bestows. At this point he is thinking of himself. Later, he will use the same terms with reference to the Philippians (verse 25) and later still (3:10-16) he will unpack the theme with reference to himself and to them. *Salvation* is therefore the better term because it does justice to what Paul goes on immediately to write about.

There are several points to consider in this massive statement of Christian experience. Taken together, they can test the genuineness and measure the quality of the experiences of Christians in this feelings-orientated age. The Bible does not merely instruct in true doctrine but also inculcates the true experience of God. In this statement there is as much doctrine as experience and they blend in terms of devotion to Christ. There are several lines of thought to be explored. We will bring these together by focusing on what Paul intends to do in his body and how he contemplates being able to do it.

The body and Paul's aims

The first matter to be considered is what Paul has to say about the body. It is important to be clear on this because the body is the sphere in which Christ is to be **exalted** (verse 20).

Paul is not using the word *soma* (body) in any metaphorical sense in this verse as he does elsewhere; e.g., 1 Corinthians 12:12ff. and Ephesians 4:4 where the church, universal and local, is depicted as being in the kind of relationship to Jesus Christ which resembles that of a body to its head.

Here Paul is speaking about his own body and refers to it simply, but most seriously, as being that in which he will do his living and dying. Clearly, the body is not only the encasement but also the means of self-expression which is an integral part of every human being.

But, the body is more than physical in the narrow sense in which that word is often understood. It is a psychosomatic entity. This means that it is not just skeleton and organs but nerves as well as muscles, emotions as well as ligaments and mind as well as brain. The body, therefore, is not just an animated complex but is an intimate part of the psyche of the whole person. The body of a human being has a greater dignity than the body of an animal simply because it is the body of a person.

There is, however, another dimension to the meaning of the term *body* in this passage. It is brought out by the use of the word *sarx* in verses 22 and 24 meaning *flesh*. Obviously, there is a large area of common meaning between the two terms because Paul equates living with living in the flesh (verse 22) and dying as not remaining in it (verse 24). But the change should be noted. Setting aside the idea that *body* and *flesh* are just synonyms, we are informed that the body is made of flesh. This is not meaningless repetition because all bodies do not have to be bodies of flesh. Paul speaks of a spiritual body in 1 Corinthians 15:44. A body of flesh is a body which is frail, subject to decay, capable of suffering illness and even death as a result of the Fall. It is a lowly body (see 3:21 and comment there). It would be better if the NIV had retained *flesh*. The term flesh has, however, a different meaning in 3:3 (see comment).

The *body* of chapter 1 is therefore the psychosomatic unity made infirm as a result of the Fall (Genesis 3:19). Because of its frailty, the person who lives in it is open to being affected in all sorts of ways. The body, with its senses, is a major area of the Christian's vulnerability. Paul's aim is, therefore, most striking for he intends that in his body, living or dying, Christ's glory is going to be manifested and not his own weakness.

Paul's helps to achieve his aim

Clearly, Paul's aim is not one which is easily achievable. The pressures of living and dying in a frail body and in a fallen world are immense. They make one realise what one is made of - or not made of! But Paul's aim was no daydream because he did not depend on his own resources to attain it. He was conscious of his need of help. That is why the verbs he uses in this section are in the passive voice - they express not what Paul is going to do, but what will be done in and for him by another.

Two channels of help are referred to, namely, the praying of the church at Philippi and the supply of the Spirit of Jesus Christ. The combining of these by means of the single preposition **through** in verse 19 is noteworthy because quite obviously a major difference exists between them. The first is human; the second is divine. There is no greater difference than that except for the divine and the demonic. Yet the human and the divine are here associated in terms of providing help as if each provided a source of the necessary aid, independent of the other. That of course is not so, not even when it is the saints and the Spirit who are being spoken of. It is rather that the prayers of the saints are being dignified by being associated with the supply of the Spirit.

Paul often refers in his letters to the prayers of the saints either by way of grateful acknowledgement or importunate request (Romans 15:30; Ephesians 6:19; Colossians 4:3,4; 1 Thessalonians 5:25; 2 Thessalonians 3:1,2). At times it seems as if the more prayer that is offered, or the more that pray, the greater is the hope of needs being supplied (2 Corinthians 1:11). But that is not the case. By praying for him, they share with him in the spread of the gospel. As they do this together and each in his place, the more delighted God is to answer favourably to the encouragement of his servants. Church prayer meetings ought to be well attended and fervently expectant. They provide a means of working in places where we cannot go, of helping those who have actually gone there and, in the process, bringing pleasure to God's heart and extension to his kingdom.

The major source of help, however, is the Spirit who is

termed **the Spirit of Jesus Christ**. The best way to understand this expression is to think along two lines. First, we
should see a reference here, not to the divine nature of Jesus
but to the Holy Spirit, the third person of the Trinity.
Secondly, we should notice that the Spirit is connected with
Jesus who is described as the Christ (Messiah). The Spirit is,
therefore, presented as the one who endued Jesus with all that
was necessary for his Messianic ministry (cf. Isaiah 11:1,2;
61:1ff.; Matthew 3:15,16; John 3:34 and Hebrews 9:14). It
was by the Spirit that Jesus of Nazareth, in that way which
was unique to the divine Messiah, magnified God in his body,
living and dying.

The bearing of this on Paul's resolve is that, just as Jesus
the Christ was helped by the Spirit in the days of his flesh, so
Paul sees the Spirit as enabling him to be what he ought, as
a Christian, in the process of living and in the act of dying.
What is more, he sees this help being provided in abundance.
The word *epichoregia*, translated **help** (NIV) was used for
the function of a ligament in the body, for the caring for a wife
and providing for a chorus in a drama. It is a dynamic term
which is related to the accomplishment of a purpose. This
being the case, the word *help* is too vague. The KJV rendering
supply is better. The ideas in the word are those of support and
endowment. The Spirit would come alongside him in the
tangled and threatening circumstances of life and provide
strength for every eventuality. Is he not the Comforter?

The resolve itself

Though Paul would attribute any success in glorifying Christ
to the aid of the Spirit, this does not mean that he regarded his
resolve and activity as being superfluous. The Spirit would
enable him to will (resolve) and to act (perform) God's good

pleasure in situation after situation, but not do it for him
(2:13).

What then does he have to say about his own part in the
whole process of glorifying Christ? We begin by drawing
attention to the word **For** which begins verse 21. This is often
overlooked but it should not be. It points out that all Paul
expectantly declares in verse 20 is the consequence of the
statement of glorious fact which he is able to make in verse
21. The logic - and spiritual experience does have a logic
about it - is that if in the context of living, Christ has become
life itself to him, so dying must be gain and nothing but gain,
because, of course, it takes him *to* Christ. Through the supply
of the Spirit of Christ, Paul is determined to be able to live or
die to Christ's glory. This is the highest statement of Christian
experience in the whole of the New Testament and every
Christian is to aspire to it. Chapter 3 will point out the way
towards this lofty goal.

Verse 20 unfold's Paul's state of mind as he looks
forward. It is noteworthy that it is entirely positive. This does
not mean that he is closing his eyes to the grim, demanding
realities of life and pretending all is well. He mentions death,
the last grim enemy. But there is not a cloud on his horizon.
He is filled with confident anticipation, reaching forward
eagerly to what he expects. Any possibility that his hopes
might be dashed and that he might be put to shame is not
countenanced for one moment. Tomorrow would be as
yesterday, whatever it might bring.

Courage is the dominant characteristic of Paul's mind
and heart. The Greek term, *parresia*, is a great New Testament word. It expresses the distinctive effect of the revelation
of God in Christ on the spirit and in the speech of those who
believe it. It is the hallmark of new covenant preaching (2

Corinthians 3:12) and witness bearing (Acts 2:29; 4:13,31). In addition to describing how Christians are able to address the unbelieving world, it is also used to express their joyful, confident approach to God himself in praise and prayer (Ephesians 3:12; Hebrews 10:19; 1 John 2:28; 3:21; 5:14). The ministry of Jesus the Christ was marked by authority in all he taught and did. That certainty is translated by the Spirit of Christ into boldness in the believer.

What gave rise to this resolve on Paul's part is his devotion to Jesus Christ which is expressed in the great statement of verse 21. It is because of the glory of Christ that he formed the resolve which he did. This well known statement also holds the key to understanding the dilemma in which he found himself and which he describes in verses 22-24. We must remember that this statement is a personal testimony. This does not mean that it can only refer to the one who made it but it would be a serious and costly mistake for anyone to think that it is automatically true of everyone who is a Christian.

Though Paul uses two infinitives in verse 21, namely, **to live** and **to die**, their tenses are different. The first refers to something ongoing, the second to an event. *To live* includes the demands and duties of daily living in a kaleidoscope of circumstances. By saying that for him living was Christ, he is declaring that he consciously relates himself to Christ in all these situations and experiences. Christ was no adjunct or occasional extra to Paul's living. *To die* refers to the actual event with all its circumstances. Paul would enter into that too, in fellowship with Christ, just as into any circumstance of living.

He was consequently torn between two options. Perhaps he was chained to two soldiers, one on either side, so that he was painfully conscious of the slightest movement of either, as some have suggested. There is nothing impossible in that. But it should not be necessary to visualise such a scene in order to do justice to the graphic language of verse 23a. It was being bound up with Christ and not being bound to his guards that made him think as he did. We must try to look into Paul's own mind and heart and see the conflicting pressures which he referred to as, in fellowship with Christ, he looked out on living and dying.

His dilemma was created because of the reality and glory of Christ to him. Since that was his perspective, there could be no uncertainty as to which was better. Dying was **better by far**, literally far, far better (a triple comparative). But that conclusion was based entirely on what would be better for him as an individual. Dying would be gain because it would take him nearer to Christ than anything in life could effect, even bearing in mind what the Spirit could supply. As a result, he would be **with Christ**. That was very much better and it would come about at the moment of death. Departing from the flesh would mean not only the laying aside of every opposition and limitation, but a face to face fellowship with Christ in heaven. Any notion of being unconscious or asleep until the resurrection day is excluded as a possibility.

On this point of being with Christ, it is worth referring briefly to what Paul had already written to the Christians at Corinth about the believer and death. In 2 Corinthians 5:1-10, he describes the believer as being naked after death. This, of course, means being disembodied, that is, without either his heavenly dwelling (the resurrection body, 2 Corinthians 5:3,4) or his earthly tent. But he also describes such a believer as being at home with the Lord (2 Corinthians 5:8). While there is much more of salvation to come to a believer than occurs at death and there is a certain incompleteness until the general resurrection, yet the believer at death is at home with Christ. There is no sleeping of the soul after death and no purgatory between death and heaven.

Only one thing was worthy of comparison to being with Christ in heaven and that was living for him on earth. That is the contrast in these verses. It is not between living and dying as they affect every Christian but as they affect a Christian for whom life truly means Christ's glory. It is between living in the body to serve Christ and leaving the body to be with him.

It is because Christ was so paramount in Paul's thinking that he was uncertain which to choose, not which was personally preferable. Christ was in view whichever direction Paul looked and the choice therefore was his, not Paul's. Living would mean **fruitful labour** on behalf of Christ among his people. Leaving would mean rest from labour and enrichment in Christ's presence. His dilemma was the result of intimate fellowship with the Christ who loved him and who loved the church. It could only be resolved by Christ either taking Paul to himself or leaving him for his church.

His inward unrest was resolved by means of a conviction being given to him. Verse 25 speaks of his being persuaded that he would remain with the church (cf. the guidance given in Acts 16:6,7). This persuasion did not overcome his reluctance but it dispelled uncertainty. It is expressed in terms which are important for an understanding of the rest of the letter. Paul was to remain for the good of others (verse 25). That is put before his own greater good. This is the mind of Christ, which is so emphasised later, being reproduced and intensified in the apostle.

Here, then, there is no love of living or fear of dying. Nor is the preference for dying which is expressed a perverse deathwish, or a desire just to be rid of the body of flesh and of a fallen world. It arises out of the same loving desire for Christ which makes Paul more than willing to live on for him. Can we rise to Paul's level in these words? Chapter 3 will point the way.

Paul had spoken about the advance of the gospel in the sure belief that the Philippians would be glad to hear of it. He had also spoken of the advance of his own salvation. Now in 1:25,26 he uses the same language with regard to the Philippians themselves. They are also to advance, in increasing joy, as they keep the faith. What this entails is made clear in the following verses. So when Paul is restored to them they will rejoice in the Lord Jesus Christ even more.

4. THE MAIN EXHORTATION SUMMARISED (1:27-30)

The expression **Whatever happens**, with which the NIV begins verse 27 is an interpretation rather than a translation of the Greek text. Sometimes, of course, it is necessary for a translator to search out an equivalent expression for a piece of text which is untranslateable as it stands. A good example of this is the opening of 3:8, as we shall see. But there is no such difficulty with regard to the opening of verse 27.

Paul uses an ordinary enough word here and a commonly used English word exists to translate it. *Monon* means *only* (cf. KJV) or even *one and only*. Using *only* instead of *whatever happens* has the effect of bringing to the fore the words which follow, underlining their importance and highlighting the distinctiveness of what they say. *Whatever happens* draws attention more to the author and to the readers, that is, whatever happens to me or to you. While Paul does go on to refer to his own and then to his readers' circumstances, we question whether that was his thinking when he used this word *monon*.

In our view, *whatever else* would do more justice to Paul's thinking at this point because what he was seeking to do was to gain attention for the exhortation which follows. *Monon* is joined to *a manner worthy of the gospel* at the beginning of the sentence. It is our view that Paul wanted to highlight this matter amid everything else he was going to say. He was summarising his message. The wood must not be lost sight of because of the trees.

What then is this great matter? It is that believers (cf. 1:1) should live in a way which is **worthy of the gospel of Christ**. But what does it actually mean to magnify Christ in the body? In short, it means to live a kind of life on earth which is totally different from that of the world. It is standing firm, being unafraid of opponents, and yet being humble (1:27; 2:3-5). It is a life of love to Jesus Christ and his people which is in keeping with the faith of the gospel. It is developing a contentment which is neither dependent on favourable circumstances nor destroyed by adverse ones (4:11ff). That is what Paul had been doing (verses 12-26) and what the Philippians should do. So must every Christian and every church.

This is no small, slight duty, easily understood and quickly accomplished. It involves immensities, namely, human beings and the gospel of Christ, and brings them into the closest and fullest relationship with each other in the context of the church and in the church's mission in the world.

With regard to human beings, the obligation specified does not only concern individual existence in all its aspects, that is, understanding, emotions, attitudes and actions, spoken and done, but also relationships with other people in the context of the fellowship of the church and in society at large. It includes life in its social breadth, so to speak, as well as in its inward depth. To that may be added the dimension of length, representing life in its duration because this obligation is never fully discharged on earth. There is always, even for the best (e.g. Paul), some way to go in becoming all that one ought to be because of and for the sake of Jesus Christ (3:8-12).

A greater reality comes to the fore with the reference to the gospel of Christ. This is to be understood in terms of Christ himself being the good news rather than what he preached. As such, the gospel is immense. He is the great mystery of godliness (1 Timothy 3:16) and unfathomable riches are found in him (Ephesians 3:8). He is the gospel because he is the Christ (the Messiah of God), appointed by God (the Father) and anointed by God (the Spirit). Jesus of Nazareth is the great Prophet and Priest-King (Hebrews 1:1-3; 5:6,10) and it is because of all that he is in these capacities that there is good news. Without a real Christ there can be no good news for sinners.

Priority of emphasis is given to this gospel in the exhortation contained in verse 27. Christians are to be conformed to, or become wholly conditioned by, the gospel and not the other way around. To live in a way that is worthy of the gospel is, of course, not to try to merit it and its grace, but to harmonise with it so as to display it to advantage, neither disfiguring it nor contradicting it by behaviour which is not in keeping with its spirit or character (cf. Matthew 10:37,38; Ephesians 4:1; Colossians 1:10). To be evangelical means more than to subscribe wholeheartedly to those doctrines which present the way of salvation. There is an evangelical life as well as an evangelical faith.

The verb which Paul uses to describe the kind of life which was appropriate to the gospel would have been very meaningful for the Philippians. It is the term from which our word *politics* is derived. It means something like *to conduct oneself as a citizen*. Doubtless, Paul chose this term deliberately, knowing how conscious and proud the Philippians were of their citizenship. What Paul is seeking to emphasise, then, is that it is the gospel, not their nationality, civic identity or the empire to which they belonged, which was to determine their conduct. An identical emphasis is found in 3:20 where he says that his and their citizenship was in heaven. Heaven is the state or realm to which they primarily belonged rather than to Philippi or Rome.

This supplies an all important perspective on the nature and content of the gospel. Clearly, it did not make it impossible for Christians to live in Philippi as citizens. If it had, they could not have been addressed as saints there or be required to live there as Christian people. But what it does demonstrate is that the gospel is a spiritual/moral message which joins those who believe it to heaven in a way which takes precedence over every earthly association. That distinction and emphasis needs to be understood by churches today and proclaimed by them. The gospel is not about an earthly kingdom, and social justice, although important (as we see in the prophets), is not its primary concern.

Is there anything in particular which Paul specifies as being worthy of the gospel? The latter part of verse 27 provides the answer to this question. Paul describes the church as he and the Lord Jesus Christ, their desires being one in this respect, (cf. 1:8) would wish it to be. Motivated and characterised by the gospel of Christ and irrespective of his presence or absence, the church is to be firm, united and fearless.

The faith of the gospel (verse 27) is a significant expression coming as it does so soon after *the gospel of Christ* at the beginning of the verse. It is no stylistic variation. It has a distinct meaning but one which complements the previous description. Notice the definite article appearing before the word *faith*. This points to the fact that *the faith of the gospel* is not faith in the gospel, that is faith in Christ, by which a person is saved (cf. verse 29). Rather, it is the cluster of connected truths about Christ which comprise and express the gospel. Paul uses *the faith* frequently when he writes to Timothy (e.g. 1 Timothy 3:9; 4:1). The substance of the gospel is who Jesus Christ is and what he has done in the saving purpose of God.

The beginning of verse 27 declares that there is an evangelical ethos for living. The conclusion of the verse makes clear that there is an evangelical creed which is to be believed. What is more, the creed has to be believed before the ethos can be practised.

The elements which make up that creed are listed in a number of places in the New Testament. It is not co-extensive with the whole counsel of God (Acts 20:27), and it does not include baptism (1 Corinthians 1:17). The former, which is all that God has revealed about his saving purpose is, of course, not only compatible with the gospel but explanatory and supportive of it. The latter testifies to its reality and reception.

The gospel creed focuses on the death and resurrection of Jesus Christ, according to the Old Testament Scriptures, as the accomplishment of salvation; and on the necessity of repentance and faith as the means by which that salvation is bestowed and received. By his death, Jesus Christ dealt effectively with sin and death and by his resurrection he brings new life. The gospel therefore must be his because there is no other saviour (Acts 4:12). This is how the New Testament speaks. Relevant passages which come from the lips of Jesus are Matthew 16:21; 26:54,56; Mark 10:45; Luke 24:25-27,46,47; and John 6:40,53. From the apostles' preaching to the world we can select Acts 2:23,24 and 20:21. Examples of the apostles' teaching of churches are Romans 4:23-25; 1 Corinthians 2:2; 15:1-5,12-20; Galatians 1:4-9; 1 Peter 2:24 and 1 John 4:9,10.

Because of this good news of Christ's atoning sacrifice and triumphant resurrection from the dead, Christians are to be zealous for the faith of the gospel. It is the church's most precious possession and sacred trust. How is she to act worthily of it?

Primarily, the church is to **stand firm** (verse 27). That is the major direction which Paul gives. It is amplified in the two verses which follow, repeated in 4:1 and it must be done **in one spirit**. Clearly, the church at Philippi was in some danger. It had its adversaries outside (verses 28b; 3:1-3,18,19). But to some degree it was vulnerable from within. As is pointed out in the Introduction, there was a lack of unity in the ranks. In order to meet the threat to the faith of the gospel from without, unity was essential. While churches have always had to cope with unfavourable reactions from the world, it has been, throughout history, internal weaknesses which have contributed more to her decline than external opposition.

It can be seen how basic this matter of unity is from the ways in which it is woven into the texture of these verses. While all the exhortations are in the plural, there is a repeated emphasis on oneness. These verses are written, then, not just to individuals, but to the church as a church. The resulting

picture is not of a bunch of energetic but undisciplined
volunteers but of a streamlined fighting unit like David's
army (1 Chronicles 12:23-40) which was like the army of
God (1 Chronicles 12:22). This unity of activity in the
furtherance of the gospel is a reflection of the oneness of the
three Persons of the Godhead in fulfilling the divine purpose.

One man, in verse 27, is another paraphrase. It renders a
term whose meaning, unlike *monos*, is difficult to fix with
precision. The original is the term *psyche* which can mean
soul, mind or self. A judgement must be made as to which is
best here and as to how it relates to *spirit* in the preceding
clause. Perhaps the term may be a pleonasm as in Acts 4:32
and 1 Thessalonians 5:23.

It is possible, however, to distinguish spirit from soul
without becoming too anatomical. *Spirit* can stand for the
higher element in human consciousness, that which is Godward
in its reference. It can therefore mean that Christians stand
firm by means of their spiritual union with God, or even by
the Spirit, understanding there to be a reference to the third
Person of the Godhead here. Soul/mind represents the human
senses and energies which are to be used to the full in effort
on behalf of the gospel. Whichever view is taken, it is clear
that a unanimity in thought, desire, and activity by word and
deed is being called for.

To *stand firm* is to adopt an essentially negative stance,
though it demands activity. It means to withstand, to refuse
to yield or conform. It refers to the soldier keeping his
position while under attack (cf. 1 Corinthians 16:13; Ephesians 6:13,14).

It is amplified in the two subordinate clauses which
follow. These present something essentially positive viz.
striving for something and being fearless and so form a

striking combination of steadfast resistance and zealous activity. A parallel is found in 1 Corinthians 15:58 where immoveability is coupled with activity. The key to understanding both couplets is, of course, that some pressures have to be resisted because they militate against the pursuit of other concerns and goals. Diversionary tactics are part of enemy strategy and are to be set aside (cf. Nehemiah 6:2-4; Matthew 4:1-11). There are times when the church must be negative in order to be truly positive. *The faith of the gospel* must be retained if *the gospel of Christ* is to be spread.

Contending as one man and **without being frightened** are graphic terms in the original and are rarely used in the New Testament. The first is borrowed from the world of the Roman arena and gives us our term *athletics*. It is also used in 4:3 and refers to a team activity. However, the defence and confirmation of the gospel and its furtherance in the world (1:7,14) is no game. In verse 30 Paul uses a closely associated term which gives us our word *agony* (cf. also Colossians 1:29; 2:1; 4:12; 1 Thessalonians 2:2; 1 Timothy 6:12; 2 Timothy 4:7; Hebrews 12:1,4 and Jude 3). The life and death struggle inherent in these terms - for the arena was not a stage - is best measured by our Lord's experience in Gethsemane (Luke 22:44). Yet they are not to be *frightened*. This word is not used any where else in the New Testament but in classical Greek it is used to describe horses which shy or bolt at sudden movements and noises. Standing firm is essential. It provides a basis for authentic, sustained evangelism in spite of all that adversaries may do in their malice and scheming.

Verse 28b contains two uncertainties on which an opinion has to be offered. First of all there is the question of the antecedent of the relative pronoun *which*. Is it the *faith* or the *fearlessness* of the Philippians? As Paul speaks of it as a sign, some *manifestation* of what is referred to is required. The term which is translated *sign* really means proof or demonstration. It is difficult, if not impossible, to regard *the faith* as the antecedent. So *which* must refer, we think, to the upholding and adorning of the faith by the Christians at Philippi.

Secondly, there is a debate as to whether the sign represents one thing to each group mentioned, that is, destruction to the adversaries and salvation to the believers; or whether it means both destruction and salvation but only to one group, namely the adversaries. The balance of opinion seems to favour the latter, as does the NIV translation. But even if this is what Paul meant, the believers would surely deduce from what Paul wrote that God was on their side.

To **be destroyed** or to **be saved** are contrasting eternal destinies. They are also equivalent in the sense that they involve the whole person for ever. One is either to be destroyed for ever or saved for ever and there is no middle ground and no exceptions. From the general context, it can be deduced that the hinge on which a person's eternal destiny turns is his or her attitude to the faith of the gospel of Christ and this is borne out clearly elsewhere (1 Thessalonians 1:9b-10; 2 Thessalonians 1:5-10).

Salvation here has the same meaning as in verse 19. It stands for all that is included in that best of all conditions - being with Christ for ever after death. It includes being completely holy and unspeakably happy, beyond the reach of temptation and sin, with saints and angels in the presence of God in heaven. By contrast, awful contrast, *destruction* is that worst of all conditions - being without Christ for ever after death. It includes being bound to one's own sin and subject to unbearable anguish and misery which nevertheless has to be borne, in the company of the wicked and of Satan and his demons, banished from Christ yet under the just punishment and wrath of God in hell (Matthew 25:41; Mark 9:43-49; Luke 16:23-36; Romans 2:3-11; Revelation 6:12-16; 20:11-15).

Destruction does not mean annihilation, either at death or after the judgement. It means loss and ruin, collapse and disintegration, uselessness for any good purpose, fit only to be cast away (cf. Matthew 9:17). It is but the final effect of sin's debasing and perverting influence on human nature, coupled with God's righteous abhorrence and just punishment of it. As the same adjective *eternal* is applied to it as to salvation (Matthew 25:46), they are equally unending. While such a prospect is awful to contemplate and difficult to conceive of, human sentiment and reasoning must not be allowed to determine this matter but God's own word. God will triumph in hell no less than in heaven.

Verses 29 and 30 enlarge a little on the matter of hardship encountered in the cause of the gospel. Some in the church would be able to remember the suffering which Paul experienced while at Philippi and here he explains what lay behind that as well as their own present difficulties. In doing so he has some important teaching to give on the matter of faith or believing. We begin with that. Two aspects need to be noted.

Faith is a gift

Though believing is something which a person does, the disposition and resolve to do so, both at the beginning of the Christian life (cf. 1:6) and throughout its course, comes from God. The verb **has been granted**, since it is in the passive mood with no subject, needs to be understood as a divine passive i.e. God is its subject. Faith is a gift of God (Ephesians 2:8).

Faith has an object

As believing is something which a person does in his heart
(cf. Romans 10:9), that is, with his whole being, its existence
may not be detected by an onlooker. But it is not only a
subjective condition. It has an object, namely, Christ. It is not
merely our faith which is a divine gift but the object of the
faith as well. Jesus, the Christ, is the unspeakably great gift
of God (2 Corinthians 9:15). He is therefore to be received
submissively as Lord and trusted in as Prophet, Priest and
King.

What then do these verses have to say about suffering? The
answer is that it is much the same as what they have to say
about faith. Suffering is a gift from God, no less than faith,
and it is also related to Christ, but not in exactly the same way
as faith is.

Suffering is a gift

The one verb **has been granted** governs both the believing
and the suffering. It is compounded from the noun *charis*
which means grace. Just as faith is a gift of God in his
graciousness and hence an immense favour and privilege, so
is suffering.

Suffering for the gospel is not pleasant and is caused by a
hostile world which opposes God and Christian people. This
can so colour one's outlook that it may be thought God ceases
to regard his people as his own, rather than bestowing an
honour upon them. The apostles Peter and John rejoiced
because they had been counted worthy of suffering disgrace
for the Name (Acts 5:41).

Suffering is for Christ

Faith has Christ for its object; that is, people trust in him, in his merit and power to save. Suffering is **for him**, that is, on account of him, the one believed in, or for his sake. Faith is not only the means by which benefit is derived from the Saviour but it incorporates or unites believers to him (cf. 3:9,10) so that they become like their Master. As the world treated him, so in principle it will treat them. It cannot be otherwise for the servant is not higher than his lord (John 15:18-21). As the world did not perceive his true identity, so it will be blind to theirs (1 John 3:1b). Seeing, however, that Christians are different from the men and women of the world, they are treated by the world as Jesus was.

There could also be a deeper meaning in these words and there probably is. Suffering for Christ is not just suffering on account of him, in the way that has just been described, but it is suffering *instead* of him. It is suffering which he would have had to endure if he were still on earth but which he has bequeathed to the church to complete. Colossians 1:24 refers to this. These are not the sufferings which only Jesus Christ could undergo, by which he bore sin's penalty (cf. John 1:29). They have been fulfilled and finished. But the sufferings referred to in this section are those which are received in the course of that same general service of God in a fallen world in which both Christ and his people engage (1 Peter 2:19-25). This is a privilege indeed, to follow in the Saviour's steps, to bear something instead of him who bore so much for us, and thus share in the fellowship of his sufferings (3:8).

5. THE MAIN EXHORTATION IN DETAIL: (2:1-18)

It is to be regretted that the NIV chooses to omit the word *therefore* from the first verse of this section. There is every reason for it to be included and even perhaps for its being the word with which this second chapter of the letter commences. It is present in the original text and serves the important and useful purpose of establishing a close connection with the immediately preceding verses which we regarded as a summary of the main exhortation of the letter. Twin emphases are found in it, namely, the unity of the church and the service of the gospel.

Those are the themes which are focused upon and expanded in the first half of this new chapter. Unity is treated in verses 1-4 and evangelism in verses 14-18. Between them is the well-known passage about the mind of Christ which is integrally related both to what precedes and to what follows it. The mind of Christ is, therefore, vital for the unity of the church and its dissemination of his gospel.

We will sub-divide this section as follows:
1. The unity of the church (verses 1-4)
2. The mind of Christ (verses 5-11)
3. The obedience of the church (verses 12-18)

The unity of the church (verses 1-4)

The Form of the Appeal

This paragraph is a heartfelt, yet skilfully constructed appeal which is firmly based and specifically aimed. The central request is **make my joy complete** in verse 2. This is not merely a request that Paul's joy might be increased. He has already declared that the Philippians have made him glad by their long-standing partnership in the cause of the gospel (1:4,5). He now expresses the desire that they might also make him glad by their harmonious unity. Clearly, Christian joy is not mindless euphoria. We would do well at this point to remember that it is not only the Lord's servants who rejoice over the unity of Christian people but also the Lord himself (John 17:21).

Paul makes his appeal on four grounds. Though all these are introduced by the word **if**, no doubt is thereby cast on the realities to which he refers. Here, as elsewhere, notably Romans 8:31b, *if* has the meaning of *since*. It is a rhetorical device so that a forceful conclusion can be drawn. That conclusion is contained in verse 2 and it is amplified in verses 3,4.

These four influential considerations are not only all introduced by the same word, they are all phrased in the same way, without verbs. They refer to great realities in the Christian revelation and being without verbs, they constitute several fixed points for serious thought, striking hammer blows on the conscience of Christian believers. Clearly, Paul composed these statements thoughtfully. As stylistic features continue in verse 3 and 4 it ought not to be thought that Paul could not have been the author of verses 5-11 because of its poetical structure (see below).

All four grounds of appeal pluck at the strings of every Christian's experience. This is deliberate on Paul's part but not unprincipled. He wants a response of heartfelt believing obedience (1:29) to the truth of his appeal and not a fit of temporary emotion.

By referring to Christ and to the Spirit he is directing the Philippians' attention away from themselves to the self-revelation of God in the gospel. Christ is the procurer of divine salvation; the Spirit is the bestower of the blessings which Christ obtained. The other terms summarise the effects in hearts and lives of the joint ministries of Christ and the Spirit (John 16:13-15). They are the consequence of being in Christ and are of the Spirit.

How are these effects to be understood? What does each refer to and can any be associated together? If so, on what basis can this be done? All these questions arise from the actual text, as each verbless clause presents some difficulty either by way of translation or in the identification of its elements. In relation to translation, a difficulty is presented by almost the first word. Should *paraklesis*, from which we get our word *Paraclete*, be translated *exhortation* or *consolation*? The NIV opts for the former meaning by its word **encouragement**, though perhaps it is seeking thus to strike a balance between the two possibilities. The Greek can carry both dimensions of meaning and a decision between them has to be made according to the context whenever some form or other of the word is used. In this setting, the next clause is helpful because, very definitely, it carries the meaning of consolation. The question, therefore, which has to be faced about the meaning of *paraklesis* is whether Paul is repeating himself for emphasis or trying to include as much as possible to leave no loophole in his appeal. In our view, the latter is the more likely. So the NIV translation stands.

The question which arises in connection with the next clause is one of identification, namely, whose **love** is being referred to? Is it Paul's for the Philippians, the Philippians for Christ, or Christ's for the Philippians? How can a decision be made on this? We suggest the following. As various pressures are being brought to bear on the Philippians in the light of the gospel in this passage, it is better to understand the love as being either Paul's or Christ's for them rather than theirs for either or both.

Can a decision now be made between those two possibilities? The NIV inserts the pronoun **his** before **love** favouring a reference to Christ. Doing this also has the effect of linking the first two clauses, but the pronoun is not in the original. Alternatively, it could be Paul's love because it was by means of his ministry that the exhortation came and the consolation as well (1:27-30), while Christ was the ultimate source of both. We incline, however, to the view that the reference is to Christ as this adds to the forcefulness of the appeal. The beginning of the exhortation, therefore, directs attention to the lordship and love of Christ.

The identity of **the Spirit** is the difficulty which is presented by the third clause. No definite article and no qualifying adjective accompanies the noun and so it may be wondered whether it can be the third Person of the Trinity who is in view. But Paul often uses only the noun *pneuma* alone where reference is made to the Holy Spirit (cf. Romans 7:6; 1 Corinthians 2:4; Galatians 3:3) and the similarity between this verse and the apostolic benediction in 2 Corinthians 13:14 also points in the direction of such an identification. The **fellowship with the Spirit** is, therefore, a participation in Christ and his benefits which the Spirit creates and continues. This is not only individual but corporate. The church begins to come into the picture at this point.

Finally, what of **tenderness and compassion**? Whose are these? Can these be understood as being connected with the Spirit just as love is connected with Christ in the second clause? In our view this is possible and is our preferred understanding because both terms are used much more often with regard to God than to man. We have already met the first in 1:8 where the primary reference is to the intense affection of Jesus Christ and Paul uses the latter almost always in relation to God. It stands for his tender mercies. The two nouns are, therefore, closely associated and can be regarded as the reality of God's great kindness in Christ, which is communicated to the believer by the Holy Spirit himself.

The exhortation, therefore, stresses the wholehearted, active commitment of the triune God to his people. Consequently, it conveys the authoritative constraint and the affectionate appeal of the Christian gospel which calls for a similar response from those who receive it.

The Content of the Appeal

What would give Paul further reason for rejoicing? In a word or two, it is that the Philippians should be **likeminded** which, translated literally, means that they should think the same. The words which follow indicate that what is in view is not uniformity of opinion but unanimity of **spirit and purpose** which results from their having the same love. This likemindedness is more psychological than cerebral. It is distinguished more by its character than its content. Those who possess this attitude, disposition or outlook think of others before themselves, in the sense of regarding them as being more important, and they serve others before themselves. It is the kind of thinking which brought the Son of God from heaven to earth, and not only to earth but to death and even to death on a cross. It should characterise every Christian.

For a church to think in this way, and that is the dimension of these verses, is impossible without the same love being shared. Love creates oneness of soul (cf. 1:27) and also oneness of outlook and purpose. It does this because it is the effect of the love of God in Christ (1 John 3:16) which consists not merely in giving and not getting, but in self-giving even to death in order to benefit others.

Verses 3 and 4 contain specific directions. Some are negative while the rest are positive alternatives. Seeing that Paul places the negative ones first we are probably to conclude that he wants to draw the attention of the Philippians to those aspects of their church life which are unworthy of the gospel and inimical to the Christlike mind which he is striving to inculcate. In each case, however, he not only sets out what is to be rejected and repented of, but something positive which is to be pursued and cultivated.

There are three unworthy attitudes. The first two are expressed in a very emphatic way. They are preceded by the categorical negative **nothing** which amounts to a total ban and again no verb is used, as in verse 1. But there is a difference of method and tone to note between those two verses. Though Paul is aiming to make his message as forceful as possible in both verses, he approaches them from the side, as it were, in verse 1, infiltrating their minds, whereas in verse 3 (and verse 4) he makes an all out frontal assault.

The attitudes which are vetoed are **selfish ambition** and **vain conceit** (verse 3) and *self pre-occupation* (verse 4) They are an unbecoming trio indeed and perhaps the last mentioned is the root of the other two. Selfish ambition has already been mentioned (cf. 1:17). It is a seeking of influence and position for oneself which shows no compunction about using even sacred things to achieve that end. Vain conceit is self-exhibition which lacks all substance and worth. It has nothing worthwhile to display and yet it thinks it has. Self-preoccupation concentrates on one's own concerns and desires. All these enthrone *self* instead of *the Christ* who thought first of others.

The positive side calls for thoughtful effort. Christians are to be on the lookout for others (verse 4) and not to think only of themselves. While they are not to be totally oblivious to their own needs, these are very definitely to occupy second place. The striking grace which is commended and necessary for all this is **humility** (NIV). We prefer the KJV rendering at this point which speaks of *lowliness of mind* simply because it indicates the connection between humility and the kind of mind which is about to be described in verses 5-11. *Humility* is basically that mentality which genuinely regards others as being more important and valuable than oneself. It is not abject servility, as the Greeks deprecatingly thought, but dignified service of others which characterises God himself.

The mind of Christ (Verses 5-11)

The words which open this section establish a close connection with what has just gone before. The kind of attitude and action to which the Philippians have been exhorted is now presented to them as being exactly the way in which the Lord Jesus Christ himself lived.

Discussion is still going on among scholars about the form and authorship of this passage. What can be agreed is that it was written in poetic style. Whether this carries with it the idea that it was part of an early Christian hymn (as is proposed for 1 Timothy 3:16) is a moot point, though hymns to Christ were sung by the early church as part of its worship. The view that Paul could not have been the actual author of this section because of its style is a wholly gratuitous assumption. No one queries that he wrote 1 Corinthians 13 which also exhibits a rhythmical style. But even if Paul were here quoting another source, the all important fact is that it is he who is doing so. These statements, therefore, come with an apostle's imprimatur and as such are sacred scripture. We must therefore treat them in the same way as the rest of the letter.

The choice of the relative pronoun *who* at the beginning of verse 6 instead of the personal name of the one referred to is only a problem to those who do not see the poem as being fully integrated into the actual setting in which it is placed. Irrespective of whether Paul composed the poem or not, the plain fact is that he deliberately introduced it at this juncture after referring explicitly in verse 5 to Christ Jesus. The pronoun which opens verse 6, therefore, binds together all that follows with Jesus who is the Messiah.

As it is not impossible that this poem was actually sung, we will use a musical analogy to consider it and view it as having two movements. The first is downward (verses 6-8) and corresponds to the humiliation of Christ; the second, upward (verses 9-11) and represents his exaltation. Very important terms are used in this section. Some of them are not found anywhere else in the New Testament. This section is a doctrinal and devotional oratorio about the Lord Jesus Christ.

The humiliation of Christ (verses 6-8)

The first movement opens, as it were, with a chord at the top end of the highest scale imaginable with Christ Jesus **being in very nature God**. There are several points to note here. First, there is the word *being*. As a present participle, it refers to a continuing existence which underlies all that is subsequently described. But coupled with what is meant by the *very nature* of God, with which it is associated, it must also include a reference to an existence which antedated all that the apostle goes on to write about. It, therefore, points to the pre-existence of the one who became Jesus.

Secondly, this existence is described in relation to deity. The words *very nature* correspond to the Greek noun *morphe* which means *form*. This has passed into the English language, for example, in the word metamorphosis. *Morphe* is used twice in this passage, once with reference to God (verse 6) and once with reference to a servant (verse 7). In the rest of the New Testament it is only found in Mark 16:12. The NIV rendering *very nature* is, therefore, something of an interpretation or dynamic equivalent. Is it an authentic rendering of what Paul meant by *morphe*?

While scholars are not completely agreed as to the precise reason why Paul (we accept the poem as being his) chose this word, as is often the case, the alternatives which they present are not mutually exclusive. This is because, on each understanding, *morphe* means something like the essential character or distinctive attributes of a person or thing. The scholarly debate about the use of *morphe* in this passage is over whether Paul was thinking of what the word meant to classical Greek philosophers or to the translators of the Hebrew Old Testament into Greek in pre-Christian times. If it were the former, then it means *that which makes a being what it is*. If the latter, it is equivalent to *glory* or *image* which, when used of God in the Old Testament, refers to a disclosure of who and what he is.

It is just not possible at the moment for anyone to demonstrate conclusively that Paul was thinking of either usage of *morphe* to the exclusion of the other. Indeed, he could have been thinking of both. As a result, one is faced with a term which refers to the pre-incarnate Christ as possessing what constitutes deity in its fullness. By his incarnation he came to acquire all that characterised servant-hood as well.

Before moving on, perhaps a plea may be entered for favouring the Old Testament association rather than the philosophical one. Two reasons in support of this may be advanced. The first is that what is biblical should always be given preference over what is philosophical. The latter can not only be abstract but speculative. The second is that relating *morphe* to glory/image and linking it to Jehovah's self revelation in majesty and condescension in the Old Testament, enables a connection to be made between Jesus Christ and that wealth of material. This may point to the reason why Paul chose the term for this passage because majesty and condescension are its focal theme. The NIV's paraphrase *very nature*, therefore, conveys well the meaning of the word *morphe*.

Verses 6-8 make up the opening movement. They concentrate attention on the lowliness of mind of the being who became Jesus Christ and go deeper and deeper into what animated him to do so. There is a perspective here which is unique in the New Testament. From other passages we learn that Jesus knew in advance what he would suffer at the hand both of his foes and of his Father (Matthew 16:21; 20:22) and yet went on steadfastly (Luke 9:51). We are also informed that he was sustained in this by the prospect of glory and joy after suffering (John 17:5; Hebrews 12:2). But what was it in the first place, that led him to be willing to come to earth to die? It is these verses in Philippians 2 which give the answer. It was his **attitude** (verse 5). This was a disposition, an affair of the heart and not merely the brain. It was charitable, not cerebral. It led him to empty himself, to humble himself. We see here how the cross appeared from all eternity to the one who was to be crucified on it.

The second half of verse 6 is the main clause of the statement and begins to record this downward movement. Two questions have to be raised concerning it.

The first concerns the meaning of **equality with God** and is rather academic. Is this a further description of the *morphe* of God or of the kind of existence which the pre-incarnate Christ knew before the creation of the world? The distinction between those two things is not a meaningless one because the former is unchangeable while the latter is not. Commentators are divided on this. Those who regard it as not being identical with *morphe* usually go on to understand it as that form of existence of which the Christ emptied himself when he came to earth. But there is another way - a better way - as we shall see of understanding the astounding expression *he emptied himself*. We therefore regard *equality with God* as being what is necessarily involved in sharing in the *morphe* of deity.

The second question concerns what is meant by **something to be grasped**. That is how the NIV translates a single Greek word which is found nowhere else in the New Testament, never in the Greek Old Testament and only rarely in secular Greek. But it is the key word in this statement. It refers either to an action of seizing, holding or robbing (KJV) or to something passive, namely, what is held or seized; for example, plunder or booty. The NIV's somewhat imprecise rendering at this point has the merit of leaving the problem for the exegete to solve rather than concealing it by a paraphrase.

What then can be said about it? So much has been written about this term that what follows is bound to be an over simplification. Still we suggest that perhaps too much attention has been given to the individual word and nowhere near enough to the other terms with which it is associated. But as there are no other uses of the term in the New Testament to consider, it is inevitable that the context must be given the decisive voice in determining its precise significance.

We begin, therefore, not with the word which causes the difficulty but its associated verb, that is, **did not consider**. It should be noted that it has already been used in verse 3. Clearly, something similar is being spoken of in the two places. The command in verse 3 is to think about others and not oneself. That provides a perspective which is near the heart of the matter focused on in verse 6, namely, that Christ did not think about something in a self-centred way. What was that something?

The basic decision which now has to be made about this **something** is whether it was already possessed by him or whether he was capable of obtaining it. Using the verb *to hold* instead of *to grasp*, the issue can be put as follows. Did the Christ choose not to lay hold of something or not to keep hold of it? When we remind ourselves that the *something* in question was that which he had from all eternity, namely, equality with God, does this not mean that *keeping hold* must be preferred to *laying hold*. Who lays hold of what he already has?

From the context, therefore, we adopt the view that what is referred to in the second half of verse 6 is that he who possessed equality with God from all eternity by virtue of his being in very nature God, did not grasp it, that is, keep hold of it. The KJV translation, *thought it not robbery to be equal with God*, presents a slightly different truth, namely, that the pre-existent Christ did not think that he was detracting from

God's glory by claiming equality with him. While that is true, what is being suggested as the precise meaning of the original is that he was not preoccupied with who he was! He was not self-regarding. In favour of this interpretation is the fact that it stands in marked contrast to what immediately follows, namely, he **made himself nothing**. What does that mean?

Before seeking to answer that question, we ought to note an interesting possibility in relation to the opening of this poem. The clause which opens verse 6 is sometimes understood and even translated concessively, that is, *although he was* ... (NASB). This has the effect of pointing out the contrast between his eternal deity and his subsequent condescension. The clause could, however, be understood in a causal sense and translated *because he was in very nature God, he did not regard equality with God as something to hold on to*. This would declare that everything which comes into the category of his self-giving is the consequence and expression of the kind of deity which belongs to him. This not only distinguishes Jesus Christ from all other so-called saviours but distinguishes the one, true and living God from all other gods falsely so called. The glorious God is as concerned for the good of others as he is for his own glory. Perhaps that is his highest excellence.

We consider now the expression in verse 7, **but made himself nothing**. The New American Standard Version translates this as he *emptied himself*. In the early part of this century that rendering was used in support of a view which, on other grounds, regarded Jesus as only human. He was regarded as having emptied himself of his deity by virtue of becoming incarnate. But that is not how the translation should have been understood, as we shall see. In any case, to conceive of one who was in very nature God deciding to cease to be God should have been a thing unthinkable.

How then should the expression *he emptied himself* be understood? It is after all the literal rendering. At the outset, we argued that the beguiling question, 'Of what did he empty himself?' should not be asked if only because the passage does not provide an answer. Instead, we should ask, 'what did it mean for him to empty himself?' Two answers *are* provided to that question in the New Testament.

The first is to see the verb as having a metaphorical sense and meaning something like *being without effect* or *counting for nothing*. That is how it is understood in the other places where the verb occurs in the New Testament (cf. Romans 4:14; 1 Corinthians 1:17; 9:15; 2 Corinthians 9:3). The NIV has taken it this way and has *making himself nothing*. This expression points to something wonderful and amazing. It declares how the one who, being in the form of God, counts for so much, discounted himself in his own reckoning for the benefit of others (cf. John 13:1-3). He was not self-regarding though he knew who he was and all that he possessed. What follows sets out how self-renouncing he became.

The second answer suggests that the expressions, **taking the very nature of a servant, being made in human likeness** and **being found in appearance as a man**, indicate what this self-emptying involved. It was not a laying aside and a leaving behind of something he had, but a taking to his divine self of something which he never had or was before, that is, a human nature. This can be termed a making of himself as nothing because of the immeasurable distance between deity and humanity, sovereignty and servanthood. That is what he resolved to do while in the form of God.

Verse 7 records the visible results of the carrying out of this resolve. We begin by considering two individual words.

They are **likeness** and **appearance**. It must be pointed out
that Paul does not use the word *morphe* in this connection.
Instead, the words he uses are *homoioma* and *schema* which
have a broad coincidence of meaning. They refer to what is
immediately recognisable to the human eye as denoting what
someone or something looks like. In these verses, they point
to the fact that the pre-existent Christ became also truly and
fully human. No one who met Jesus of Nazareth would have
had a second thought about his humanity (or about his
masculinity for that matter). It was his deity which they failed
to see and that is the *morphe*.

The term *homoioma* (likeness) is used in two ways in the
New Testament. It can either refer to an identity or to a
similarity and once more the setting must decide which. In
Romans 8:3 the expression *likeness of sinful man* is found and
that must point to similarity, because Jesus knew no sin and
committed no sin (2 Corinthians 5:21 and 1 Peter 2:22). In
Hebrews 2:17 and 4:15 an identity is the appropriate meaning
because it is flesh and blood and temptation which are in view.

In verse 7, the term is linked with **being made**. As this is
a reference to his birth, likeness rather than identity is
appropriate because his conception was unique, being 'Con-
ceived of the Holy Ghost and born of the Virgin Mary'. His
resultant humanity was real and finite like ours, but without
sin which was no part of human-ness as originally created.
Being found in appearance as a man refers to what a glance
declared him to be, namely, fully and truly human. His
human-ness was physical, consisting of a body with its needs;
and also psychological, that is, a reasonable soul with thoughts,
emotions and resolutions. What is more, it was human nature
in its frailty. It was thus different from both the animal and,
one presumes, from the angelic but it was not incompatible

with the divine! What the first movement in this poem asserts is that servanthood and human-ness are both equally, harmoniously and gloriously true of the same being who had been fully divine before his incarnation and remained so during and after it.

He humbled himself and became obedient indicates that servanthood was the hallmark of the earthly life of the man, Jesus Christ. He resolved wholeheartedly to become a servant and to become a man. His self-abnegating choice lay behind his becoming each and both together, by virtue of his incarnation. The eternal Son of God was born of a woman and made under the law (Galatians 4:4,5). So we have the God-Man in the status of a servant. The opening clause of verse 8 refers to the full reality of that human-ness which the divine person united with himself, while the rest of the verse points to what servanthood in that human condition entailed for him. He involved himself in the same living and dying process as Paul did (1:20ff).

In verses 7 and 8 the main emphasis is on servanthood. That is what is mentioned first in verse 7 and last and more fully in verse 8. This does not mean that human-ness is underplayed. On the contrary, it is highlighted by the words **as a man** which indicate that becoming human was essential for rendering the service which was required of him. In other words, he became human in order that he might become capable of being obedient unto death. Salvation is not just by means of the union of human nature with the divine in the person of the Son of God, but particularly through his subsequent perfect obedience.

The question of what kind of servanthood Paul is thinking of at this point has now to be considered. There are two possibilities. The first is the Servant of the Lord in Isaiah 40-

55. The second is the first century slave. In favour of the first possibility is the suggestion that Paul alludes in verse 10 to Isaiah 45:23. In favour of the second possibility is that Paul is calling Christians to think of the needs of others and not their own rights. This was true of the first century slave who had no rights at all. If Jesus became a slave in that sense, that is, he forewent all that he could insist on for himself, then the exhortation gathers greater strength. It ought to be borne in mind, however, that as the Servant of the Lord gave up his independence to do the will of Jehovah (Romans 15:3), there is not that much of a clear distinction between the two interpretations.

The expression **he humbled himself ... to death** presents a vital perspective on the obedience of Jesus Christ. The preposition *to* really means *until* and denotes much more than a point of termination. We have the picture of additional, more costly, acts of self-abnegation being required of Jesus than even his incarnation, as he went further down the path from the manger to the cross. This describes his service as something ongoing and increasing; something living and ultimately life-consuming in that it only comes to an end with life being expended in death. 'Not my will but thine be done' (Luke 22:42) summed up his life (cf. John 8:29). He was to live as a servant before God with the whole of his being and for the term of his natural life, from womb to tomb. He learned what was actually involved in obeying by the things which he suffered (Hebrews 5:7-9).

Verse 8 concludes with the emphatic words **even death on a cross**. The Lord did not merely humble himself to die but to die on a cross. Clearly there is something special about this. Obviously much more is included in this expression than the form of execution which he underwent. After all, he was not the only one to be crucified. The cross stands for the kind of death which he died, viewed from both the Roman (Gentile) and Jewish standpoints. There is nothing sacred or valuable about the actual wood of the cross.

What then was unique about the death which Jesus died on Golgotha? From the Roman angle, crucifixion was the method of capital punishment usually reserved for the lowest of the low. No Roman citizen could be crucified. When Jesus was crucified, two rebels, thieves and murderers, were put to death with him, by the authority of Pontius Pilate. All three were crucified alive. So Jesus was despised and rejected by men in his death. To die on a cross was to become 'one from whom men hide their faces' (Isaiah 53:3). It was to become 'a worm and not a man, scorned by men and despised by the people' (Psalm 22:6). To die on a cross, therefore, was to be despised and rejected of men.

But what did death on a cross mean to a Jew? Something worse - far worse. Crucifixion was not a Jewish form of capital punishment. That was usually by stoning (cf. Acts 7:59). But corpses were hanged on a tree (cf. Deuteronomy 21:22). This was to indicate that the death which had been inflicted was death under the curse of God. Jesus was, therefore, rejected and accursed by God and that was far worse than all that human beings could inflict. He was forsaken by God and punished by him in body and in soul, experiencing the displeasure and damnation of God due to sinners. He was 'stricken of God' (Isaiah 53:4). It 'was the LORD's will to crush him and cause him to suffer' (Isaiah 53:10). That was what death on a cross meant - being rejected and abhorred, abused by men and accursed by God. For one who was still in the form of God to give himself up to such treatment by men is staggering. For him to do so with reference to God and for God to treat him in such a way is beyond words.

But why did it happen? Some have pointed out that Paul makes no connection between Christ's death and sins in this passage. While that is true, two things need to be said on that score. The first is that in 3:18,19 there is a definite connection between the cross of Christ and a sinful outlook and conduct. The latter contradicts the purpose of the former. Christ died to redeem from iniquity. Secondly, it is clear that his death came within the scope of obedience to God. It is only the fact that this suffering was the climactic part of the obedience required of him that prevents the cross of Jesus from being the ultimate obscenity. He put himself under the law for others who had broken it and so he was being treated by God as those transgressors ought to have been treated. While this expressed God's justice, it also revealed his love - in his giving of his Son and in the Son's giving up of himself to the Father's will for the well-being of others. It is to such a disposition that Christians are called. The attitude of Jesus Christ is not merely to be admired by them or meditated on but copied, fleshed out in self-sacrificial lives.

The exaltation of Christ (verses 9-11)

This is the second and final part of what has been described as a theological oratorio (see page 67). It is not, however, in the form of a progressive movement as the first was. But it could have been. Paul could have spoken about how Christ, after death, rose again the third day, ascended into heaven, sat on the right hand of God from whence he will come to judge the living and the dead. But he did not do so. Why not? The reason for the downward progression being detailed in the previous verses was doubtless because it exemplified the insistent and increasing attitude of Christ Jesus which Paul was concerned to present to the Christians at Philippi. As what follows does not do that, it does not follow the same pattern of presentation.

But why then have a further part at all? Why not end the poem with verse 8? After all, the first part has both validated the basis of the exhortation (cf. *in Christ* in verse 1) and expanded on its content (cf. *humility* in verse 3). Why not leave the matter there?

Two reasons can be suggested as to why Paul did not do that, indeed could not do that. The first relates to the need of the Philippians themselves. Verses 9-11 record the action of God by way of response on his part to the life and death of Jesus Christ. The word **Therefore** at the beginning of verse 9 makes that clear. Something further is being said to the Philippians about the humility and obedience to which they are being exhorted, namely, that it is of great worth in the sight of God.

Secondly, verses 9-11 relate to Jesus Christ himself. We have suggested that Paul could not have written what he did about the humiliation of Jesus Christ without being moved to speak of his exaltation. It is in a sense inevitable that he should want to continue that sacred history which he has been relating. Having traced it from its heights to its depths, he takes it up to the heights again. It just could not be left at its lowest point.

How does he do so? What is the form of this final movement? It is not a measured upward progression to a climax. It is the climax itself. Paul gathers together the resurrection, ascension, intercession and heavenly session of the Lord Jesus Christ. It is a crescendo focused on the exaltation of Jesus Christ in heaven and on the last day.

While these verses do not present technical difficulties of

the kind found in the previous section it would be a mistake to think that they are easily understood in all their rich significance. Several theological matters call for attention. The first two relate to the connection between the truth taught in the two parts of the poem. This connection is indicated by the word *therefore*.

First, the exaltation described in these verses corresponds to the humiliation of the first part: death on a cross means the most abject humiliation; the exaltation is **to the highest place**. Paul was fond of superlatives and would become exuberant when speaking of Jesus Christ and the gospel. We have already met with an example of this in chapter 1 when he declared that being with Christ was not only better than serving him on earth, but better by far. Verse 8 of chapter 3 provides another example. Here Paul affixes the preposition *huper* (hyper in the English language) to the verb *to exalt*. Elsewhere in the New Testament the simple verb is enough to describe the same realities (Acts 2:33 and 5:31).

It is difficult to render the compound verb by a single English verb and so the NIV has **to the highest place**. The KJV has *highly exalted him* which is perhaps better because in the context it is to a name and not to a place that Jesus the Messiah is exalted. The point to note, however, is that the degree of the exaltation is in proportion to the humiliation, though, of course, neither can be quantified in terms of human measurement.

But implicit in this correspondence is the idea of reward. The exaltation is obviously chronologically subsequent to the suffering, but it is also consequent upon it as an appropriate or a just reward.

The suffering of Jesus Christ was in the nature of obedience and the reward is the appropriate and promised consequence for his having done the work which he had been given to do. There is a corresponding *therefore* in Jehovah's prediction about the Messianic servant in Isaiah 53:12 and it is followed by an explanatory *because*. In this way, it matches the verse under consideration. Jesus prayed on this basis (cf. John 17:1-5). The notion of reward underlines the real worth of the obedience of Jesus Christ in the estimate of God.

We come finally to examine what is said about **the name that is above every name**. To be given a name may, to a western mind, not amount to very much at all. What's in a name? A rose by any other name would smell as sweet. However, to a Hebrew/Jew, a name was not an appendage to a person like a telephone number. It was an intrinsic part of the person who bore it and, by its meaning, revealed something about that individual. For a name to be given to Jesus Christ indicates that a new dignity, status and function have been given to him.

The material question, therefore, is, 'What is the name?' The passage does not provide an obvious answer to that question but it can be deduced from what is said. Two suggestions have been made. The first is that it is the name **Jesus** (verse 10). But that is almost impossible to argue because that was the name he had been given at birth. Its meaning reveals the purpose he was to accomplish, namely, to save his people from their sins. But that relates to the first part of this poem, the stage of humiliation. What is wanted now is a name which relates to his exaltation. The name in question must be **Lord** (verse 11).

For the full meaning of that name we have to remember how *kyrios* was used in the Greek speaking world of the first century. It was used as a polite form of address, an equivalent to *Sir*, as in Matthew 21:30. It was also used by Greeks to refer to one or other of their gods and, more importantly, by Greek speaking Jews to refer to Jehovah. *Kyrios* translates *Jehovah* in the Greek Old Testament.

With all that in mind, we need to examine this passage for any clues as to how the name should be understood in relation to Jesus Christ. To raise the question is almost to answer it because Jesus has already been described as *being in very nature God*. The first two uses of *kyrios* just enumerated are, therefore, to be set aside. We are then left with the Lord-Jehovah association. Is there anything in the text to support it?

Three facts can be pointed out. The first is the expression **the name that is above every name** which must mean *being above every being* because of the significance of *name* as already described. Secondly, a universal supremacy is accorded to Jesus and that belongs to deity alone. Thirdly, and most importantly, Isaiah 45:23-25 is used in this passage. The God who declared, 'I am the LORD, that is my name' (42:8), repeatedly asserts in the context of the verses just referred to, 'I am the LORD, there is none else' (45:5,18,21). The bestowal by God of his own name on Jesus means that Jesus, the man, is exalted and consequently rules over all. All authority in heaven and earth is his.

With regard to what is said about the recognition of the deity and sovereignty of Jesus, two matters have to be considered. The first is who will give it and the second, of what kind it will be.

With regard to the first matter, we have to realise that verse 10 contains three adjectives which, though they function as nouns, do not have the same power of identification which nouns possess. To render them literally would yield something like *heavenly, earthly and under the earthly*. In addition they may be neuter or masculine in gender, that is, for example *heavenly beings* or *things*. If they are neuter, that is, *things*, they are metaphorical in their meaning. They stand for all that is created and the meaning is that everything as well as everyone will acknowledge the lordship of Jesus (KJV). But if they are masculine, the reference is to rational beings only. The NIV takes this option which is to be preferred because only rational beings can be said to **bow** and **confess**. It is asserted, therefore, that all beings other than deity, that is angels, humans and demons will acknowledge that Jesus is Lord.

But what kind of acknowledgement will this be? Some argue that it will not actually take place at all because verse 10 could begin with an *in order that* instead of just a simple **that**. If that translation were to be adopted one would be left with a statement of the divine intention in exalting Jesus which, some commentators then argue, may not be realised. Since the whole passage speaks of triumph and conquest as well as universal rule, to conceive of the idea of such sovereignty being unrecognised is quite alien to the context. There will be no unsuppressed rebellion in hell. In any case the notion of God's ultimate intention being thwarted cannot be entertained by any Christian.

Whichever translation is adopted (*in order that* or *that*), the event referred to will take place. But the next question to face is what kind of recognition is being spoken of? The language of *bowing the knee* and *confessing*, which is used here, stands for worship in the Old Testament. Is that possible? Does it not then mean that if all worship, all will be saved? It is in order to avoid a sentimental and unbiblical universalism that some regard these verses as not really teaching that all *will* worship. The question becomes, 'Is there some way of avoiding both universalism and an eternal refusal to recognise Jesus as Lord which also does justice to the language of bowing and confessing?'

The way to approach this is via Isaiah 45:23b, because that is the verse which is being quoted at this point. It gives a clue as to what kind of recognition was being predicted. In verse 23 Jehovah resolves on oath to secure the submissive acknowledgement of all to himself, throughout all the nations. That excludes as a possibility the idea of recognition not being secured. Verse 24 then speaks of two groups who come to him. There are those who come in faith and are accepted and glorified and those who have raged at him who will be put to shame. The worship will mean recognition by some; adoration by others.

The emphasis in these verses is a statement that those gathered before the judgement seat of Christ will be unable to do anything other than recognise that Jesus is who God has declared him to be. This recognition is not primarily concerned with their own eternal bliss or woe, but with the glory of God the Father.

The obedience of the church (verses 12-18)
The apostle now reverts to exhortation. There are three imperatives in this section, namely, **continue to work out** in verse 12; **do** in verse 14 and **be glad and rejoice** in verse 18. While the second and third of these can be understood as parts of the first, which is more general in its scope of reference, it is important that all three are seen to be related to verse 27 of chapter 1. In other words, they describe the kind of conduct which is appropriate to the gospel.

It is the references which Paul makes to himself in this section which establish the connection with what has gone before. In verse 12 he again speaks about his being absent or present and in verses 17 and 18 of the possibility, which he cannot totally exclude, of his being taken from them. These exhortations are, therefore, to be considered in connection with the reality of eternity. Whatever happens to him, they are to live as becomes the gospel. The deduction which can be made from this is that while ministers and leaders are of great value to the church, believers ought to be faithful even if they were to be removed.

We will consider each of these exhortations in turn and the associated material. The sub-divisions of the section are fairly obvious. They are:

1. Work out your own salvation (verses 12,13)
2. Do everything as children of God (verses 14-16)
3. Rejoice even if Paul is put to death (verses 17,18)

Work out your own salvation (verses 12,13)
It should be obvious that there is an important connection between these two verses. The preposition *for* at the beginning of verse 13 which means *because* points this out. But in addition the word *work*, which is found in each of the verses, also binds them together. Christians are called upon to work out because God is at work within them. There is an element of encouragement in this but also a note of obligation. The fact that Christians are not left unaided in this work increases their responsibility to co-operate with God.

But what does **work out your salvation** mean? The NIV's inclusion of the word **continue** is due to the fact that the imperative in this verse is in the present tense. It refers to something which is of an ongoing nature. This is not the work of a day; it is the task of a lifetime.

Almost all of the appearances in the New Testament of this verb *to work out* are found in Paul's letters. It means *to bring about* or *produce* and Paul uses it in connection with both bad and good effects. An example of each is found in 2 Corinthians 7:10,11 which presents the effects of false and true repentance. Nowhere else in the New Testament is *salvation* referred to as a result of this activity. This is, therefore, a most striking use when it is remembered how often Paul describes salvation as a *gift* of God. What can this exhortation mean?

One possibility which has gained favour in recent times is to understand the salvation referred to as being equivalent to the spiritual well-being of the Philippian church. The exhortation then conveys the meaning of doing what is for the good of the church. This interpretation avoids the seeming conflict between gift and work referred to above. We must consider this a little.

The verb which is associated with the noun *soteria* does have a range of meaning in the New Testament. This means that *to save* does not always mean *to save from sin*. For example, it is often used to refer to deliverance from illness, that is, the banishing of disease or disability, with the wholeness which results from that (cf. Mark 5:23,28). Similarly, the noun may refer to release from prison (cf. 1:19 and comment there). It is, therefore, not linguistically impossible for it to refer to the spiritual wholeness (harmony and usefulness) of a church. In support of this interpretation it can be pointed out that what was threatening the church was an individualistic concern with one's own well being.

Though the older view is adopted in this commentary i.e. that there is here a reference to personal salvation, it ought not to be thought that the importance of the churchly dimension is being ignored, let alone denied. It is important in that the letter was written to the whole church (1:1) whose unity was being threatened by self-centredness (2:1-4). The question is really whether an individual's pursuit of his or her salvation *must* be out of keeping with the mind of Christ and the good of the church.

While it has to be admitted that it may be, and often has been, it must be denied that it *has* to be. Does the pursuit of one's own salvation necessarily conflict with the well-being and usefulness of the church? Is it not conceivable that if more Christians did the former in an authentic manner, that is, in accordance with the mind of Christ, the church would be a better place to be and more effective in the world as well? There is, therefore, no *necessary* conflict between the older view and the matter of considering others which the context seeks to drive home.

Two other arguments may be presented in support of the older interpretation. The first is that the noun *salvation* has already been used in this letter (cf. 1:19,28) and in both places the salvation of individuals is in view rather than of a community. Indeed, it is arguable that this is invariably the case whenever the noun is used in the New Testament. Secondly, if Paul were thinking of the well-being of the church, he could have made his meaning clearer by using another of his favourite expressions, namely, *one another*. He used that in verses 3 and 4. On the other hand, he could not have said to each individual **work out your salvation** in any other way.

Proceeding on the basis that salvation means the full conformity of the believer to Christ in spirit and in body in heaven (3:10,20,21), we must examine the meaning of the verb *work out* in that connection. It is possible that a wrong deduction may be made from the word *out* in this rendering, particularly if it is contrasted with the emphasis on *working in* found in the next verse. The activity which is called for in verse 12 is not of an external as distinct from an internal kind, but one which produces certain effects. *Work at* or *Work to* might, therefore, be more accurate because the emphasis is on the intensity and goal of the activity. The fullness of salvation does not come about apart from the energetic activity of the believer (cf. 3:10-12).

This activity is described as obedience, the essence of which must be doing another's will rather than one's own. This is God's will which is expressed in his word. The term Paul uses, *eudokia*, would be better translated by *good pleasure* (AV) rather than **purpose** because it expresses what God desires of and for his people rather than what he decrees. This note is expressed in Paul's affectionate address to the Philippians as **my dear friends**. This obedience is not forced. It is a response to the divine love.

It is also to be characterised by **fear and trembling**. Those two words are often bracketed in Scripture. They refer to the awe and reverence which is appropriate for sinners to experience in the presence of the great God who is, who speaks and who acts (cf. Exodus 15:16; Psalm 2:11; 1 Corinthians 2:3; Ephesians 6:5). 2 Corinthians 7:15 is a good example of what is referred to in this text because it combines obedience with fear and trembling. What is described there is the way in which the Corinthians regarded Titus because he was the bearer of Christ's word through the apostle Paul. So here, the believers at Philippi are to respond in the same spirit to Christ's word to them through Paul. The gospel does not cancel out all fear of God - only that which has to do with punishment (1 John 4:18) and is incompatible with God's love. There is a fear which is true reverence which the gospel intensifies. It is to condition loving, Christian obedience. Fun is not the hallmark of the Christian life.

At this point a difficulty might arise in our minds as to how a salvation, which has already been described as divine in its entirety (cf. 1:6), can be the result of activity which is genuinely human. A contradiction might seem to be inescapable at this point but the statement in verse 13 resolves it by making two things quite clear. The first is that the human activity which has been called for is not *only* human, that is, to the exclusion of the divine. God is involved in it as well. Secondly, human activity in every walk of life is made up of a decision and its corresponding action. That is also true of the Christian life as the expression **to will and to act** makes clear. But it is God who prompts and enables in both respects and, since the primary activity is his, grace is still supreme. There is a very full reference to God at this point which is not brought out in English translations. What Paul wrote was *the One who works mightily in you is God*. What believers must do is to co-operate with God in order to please him.

One further comment ought to be made, namely, that it is to those in whom God has begun a good work that this exhortation is directed. There is, therefore, an initial work in the human heart which is entirely the work of God. No co-operation is asked for in connection with that because, among other reasons, none could be forthcoming. But God does not do everything beneficial for his people apart from their activity. What he does, however, is to do everything good within them and to use their responsive activity for their own good as well as for his glory.

Do everything as children of God (verses 14-16)
This exhortation should be regarded as pursuing the thrust of
the more general one which has preceded it. The attention of
the believers is concentrated on that area of the life of the
church which needed to be amended and improved. The duty
which it specifies is that everything which falls within the
scope of Christian obedience should be done in a particular
way and for a particular purpose. The duty is related to
sanctification; the task is mission or evangelism. There is a
vital connection between the two. The Head of the church
moved on easily from praying about the church's holiness
before God to its mission on his behalf in the world (John 17:
17-18).

Before we look at the meaning and inter-relationship of
the terms which are used in these verses, we draw attention
to the possibility that Paul had in mind an incident from the
history of the children of Israel in the wilderness when he
wrote these words. Verse 5 quotes from Deuteronomy 32:5
and the reference to murmuring and disputing harks back to
incidents such as are recorded in Exodus 15:22-27; 16; 17:1-
7. We will look more closely at how the apostle makes use of
this material later but, for the present, we note the general
point from what he says: he regards the recorded history of
the people of God as being relevant not only to the church but
also to the unbelieving world. That provides a useful guide-
line for preaching from the Old Testament.

We begin, then, with the reference to **complaining** and
arguing which opens a window on the church at Philippi.
Does this refer to an expressed attitude against God, that is,
grumbling against his dealings and questioning his promises? Or is it merely to unrest and squabbling among the
believers? The former is a possibility because that is what

Israel did in the Old Testament accounts which lie behind this passage, even though there is no evidence in the letter to the Philippians that the church was guilty of that sin.

There is, however, the interesting possibility that even if the unrest were within the fellowship itself, it could still be regarded as being against God. That is because it was, in part at least, directed against the leaders of the church as was the case in the relevant Old Testament passages with reference to Israel and Moses. The support for this possibility is slight, namely, what *may* lie behind what is said to the Philippians about Timothy and particularly Epaphroditus in the next section. Whether this was true of the church at Philippi or not is a moot question. It is, however, something which often happens in churches today and is therefore a needed emphasis. Perhaps it is sufficient to think that what is in view in the verse is criticism and squabbling among the members of the church.

In seeking to examine how Paul uses Deuteronomy 32:5 in this passage we begin by looking at that chapter, which records the Song of Moses. In its opening verses, the perfection of Jehovah is rehearsed and then, by contrast, the generation of Moses' day which he declares to be no longer his (i.e. God's) children. At this point the NIV's translation **to their shame** is better rendered by *Because of their defect* (NASB) or *blemish*. Then Moses proceeds to describe the blemish of his contemporaries in terms of their being a warped and crooked generation.

There are two important things to note about the way in which the apostle uses this material in the verses under examination. They can be seen most clearly from the way in which Paul divides up the children and the generation terminology. In Deuteronomy they described the same people; not so in Philippians. The term **generation** and what is said about it is applied to the unbelieving world and not to the church. The church is described as the **children of God** and Paul holds out before them the possibility and importance of their becoming blemish-free.

What is the significance of this splitting of the Old Testament terminology? It indicates that the church of Jesus Christ has taken the place which belonged to national Israel in the purpose of God and, being made up of God's children, is capable of manifesting a likeness to God and performing a task for him in the world which Israel of old never did or could. In addition, unbelieving Gentile as well as apostate Jew are under the judgement of God and need to have the word of life which has been entrusted to the church. This shift is the result of the coming of the Messiah.

This highlights the distinctiveness of the church but also the seriousness of her calling. The actual exhortation which verse 14 begins is followed in verse 15 by a description of how the character of the church leads into her mission in a needy world. Those who comprised the church at Philippi were to become **blameless and pure** by complying with the exhortation just given. This does not amount to a call for sinlessness but for a lifestyle which displays no obvious fault because of the life which exists and flourishes in the heart. Anything to the contrary is a great hindrance in the way of effective evangelism. The world is full of criticism and complaints and a happy, trusting, loving spirit very often opens up a door for the gospel.

The description of human society in sin which is presented in verse 15 is sad but true. At times it can assume frightening proportions as in our own day. Those who belong to this way of life are declared to be **crooked and depraved**. *Crooked* points to a person's being out of line in thought, word and deed, in relation to God's law and their own nature as originally created. God made mankind upright but men have gone in search of many schemes (Ecclesiastes 7:19), that is, for other values and aims in living. *Depraved* renders a term which means to pervert or distort what is true and good with reference to oneself and to others. The New Testament example of what is in view here is Elymas the sorcerer (Acts 13:10). The picture painted by these words is not merely one in which truth is rejected, but so distorted as to seem to be falsehood, and goodness regarded as evil (cf. Isaiah 5:20,21).

This is the result of the fact that human beings are darkened and dead. That is implied in these verses by what is said about the church (**stars**) and the church's message (**the word of life**). The darkness that is in view here is both of a moral and an intellectual kind. It is the darkness of unbelief which excludes God and his word from the process of thinking about life and its mystery. Closely associated with this absence of understanding is spiritual deadness which means having no fellowship with God at all (see Ephesians 4:17-19).

In such an environment, the church is to stand out as being different and to hold out **the word of life**. What has been said about the world's corruption and ignorance and the duty of the church is plainly reminiscent of the Lord's own words about his followers being salt and light in a decadent and darkened society. Paul uses the illustration of *stars in the sky* to depict this. The NIV translation **the universe** lacks the definite article in the original and so the usual rendering *the world* is inappropriate. *Sky* is not only more accurate but more graphic because it underlines the importance of *shining*. The preceding words explain the simile.

In order for light to be brought into the world's darkness,

the church must **hold out** the word of life. Two points call for comment here. The first relates to the meaning of the verb, because there is real uncertainty as to whether it means *holding out to* or *holding on to* (cf. the NIV footnote). The decision on this will have to be made according to what one judges Paul is thinking about in this clause which begins verse 16. If he is thinking in evangelistic/missionary terms then *holding out* will be preferable; if he is thinking of the hostile and alien world in which the church is to serve her Lord, *holding on to* will be appropriate. Perhaps the fact that in verses 17,18 Paul is thinking of the possibility of martyrdom in the cause of Christ indicates that *holding on to* is the better rendering. However, if the church ceases to *hold on to* the gospel, it has nothing of real value *to hold out* to a needy world.

The word of life is the gospel of Christ by another name. Because the gospel is about Christ (see comment on 1:27), it contains and gives life. Jesus Christ is the living and life-giving word (revelation) of God (1 John 1:1-3). This life is eternal, that is, abundant, heavenly and everlasting (John 10:10,28). It alone deals with a sinner's spiritual deadness which is manifested in a life of ignorance and iniquity. The use of the term *word* here means *message*. The gospel has to be communicated in words, it is not a picture, a tune, a mime or a dance. It is a message. It is built for proclamation and that has to be in keeping with the character of the message (cf. 1 Corinthians 2:1-3).

We are now in a position to sum up Paul's desire for the church. He wants to see believers united in heart and mind, caring for each other as they obey the Lord, particularly as they co-operate in making known the gospel. This is indeed a noble aim. But it is not the totality of his vision. He does not only want to see that aim realised on earth and to experience joy as he learns that it is so. He wants to see it brought to light in heaven and to be able to boast there on account of it. Is that entirely laudable?

The word which is rendered **boast** by the NIV in verse 16 has been used before by Paul in this letter. It is found in 1:26 and there the NIV uses the word **joy** to translate it. It is clear from this variation that the term does not have to be translated *boast*, though the simple term *joy* would often not be adequate as a translation. The term means something like *to exult* (KJV has *rejoice* at this point and NASB *cause to glory*). Either of these terms would deal with the unease that Paul might be guilty of an improper boasting.

Actually, the Greek word that is used here does not refer to the act of boasting at all but to the reason for it. When this distinction is made the NIV rendering can be allowed to stand. Paul's boast is based on the Philippians living in a manner worthy of the gospel and that cannot be improper. He has already ascribed to God the glory for all that is done through them as well as in them (cf. 2:13).

But what of the reference to his own ministerial activity? Is that as easily dealt with? Well, what does he boast about in that connection? The answer is that it was not of anything which he had achieved by means of all his energetic activity. It is true that the term **run** which he uses to describe his ministry (cf. 1 Corinthians 9:24,26; Galatians 2:2), was borrowed from the world of the athletic games and was connected with effort to gain success, but all that he says about his effort is that it was not in vain. It was not fruitless. This is no more false modesty than it is self-congratulation.

It is an expression of gladness that his desire to be of some use in the service of Jesus Christ has been fulfilled. Furthermore, he thinks of his boasting as taking place on the very day when he will have to give an account, that is, **the day of Christ** (1 Corinthians 3:12ff.; 2 Corinthians 5:9,10) and God will complete his work (See comment on 1:6,10). On that day, Paul and the church will find reasons for gladness in each other in the presence of Christ (cf. 2 Corinthians 1:14) but all glory will be given to God. This cannot be selfish boasting.

Rejoice even if Paul is put to death (verses 17,18)
The third exhortation is to be joyful. In this letter, Paul frequently emphasises the importance of gladness, culminating in the well known and much quoted command *Rejoice in the Lord always. I will say it again: Rejoice* (4:4). There is, however, something unexpected or surprising about this command as presented in these verses because it is connected with Paul's death. Having referred to the coming day of Christ and his ministerial labours in that connection, he faces once more the possibility that he will be put to death. The supreme effort, the last push to glory will be required of him. In that event, he is determined to be exultant and commands the Philippians to react in the same way when they hear the news.

Paul selects the imagery of **a drink offering** at this point because it enables him to relate his life offered in death both to God and to the Philippians. This is because libations were offered along with other sacrifices. Numbers 15:3-10 makes this clear. Paul's thinking is that, though he may never be re-united with the Philippians on earth, he wants them to regard his departing as a drink offering which accompanies the primary offering of their lives in sacrificial service to God.

The use of the terms **sacrifice** and **service** in connection with faith is worth exploring a little. Their Greek equivalents occur frequently in the Greek Old Testament in connection with the activities of the priests and Levites. *Sacrifice* obviously relates to whatever was offered to God and the term *service*, which gives us our word *liturgy*, describes what took place in connection with sacrificial activity and other aspects of the worship of Jehovah. These two words *sacrifice* and *service* can be regarded, therefore, as a kind of summary of worship as connected with the tabernacle and the temple.

Their use here is significant because apart from a few references to Jewish practice in the Gospels and Hebrews, these terms are not often found in the New Testament as descriptions of Christian worship. This is because of the new order which came into being with the coming of Christ (Hebrews 9:10b). However, they are used of Christ's death and his consequent intercession (Ephesians 5:2 and Hebrews 8:6). The few uses of these terms in the New Testament are not set in a cultic context and they are not restricted to ceremonial activities. They apply to all Christians and to the whole of their lives. There are no clergy-laity and no ceremonial-secular distinctions in the new covenant. All Christians are to offer spiritual sacrifices (cf. Romans 12:1 and Hebrews 13:15-16). This does not only involve prayer, praise and the proclamation of the word, but also material gifts of some kind or other, for his needy people (2 Corinthians 9:12) and to his servants (Galatians 6:6; Philippians 4:18).

What, then, is the connection of all this with faith? The NIV understands the statement to mean that faith is the generating impulse of such acts of believers. While faith is essential before anything offered to God can be acceptable to him (see Hebrews 11:6), it may be wondered whether that is what is intended at this point. Faith is related to both sacrifice and service and can be regarded as being itself described by those words. This means that faith, that is, *believing*, is in the nature of sacrificial service. It is worship of God. It is not merely assent but submission and a submission which is characterised by devotion. In this verse it summarises the whole of the life of the church at Philippi in terms of its significance before God.

6. MINISTERIAL MOVEMENTS AND FUTURE RELATIONSHIPS: (2:19-30)

At first sight, it might seem as if this section of Paul's letter has no real connection with what precedes or follows. In addition, because Paul usually locates the kind of material which it contains either at the beginning or the end of his letters, some have concluded that it is either out of place or that its inclusion is due to no greater reason than that Paul decided to alter his usual arrangement. All such ideas are, however, well wide of the mark. They founder because they rest on the notion that there was a haphazardness about Paul's thinking. We must never forget that the mental processes of writers of Scripture were informed by the enlightening ministry of the Holy Spirit of truth and order.

What then can be said by way of explanation about the inclusion of such material at this juncture? To begin with, it needs to be admitted that there is a difference between the layout of Philippians and Ephesians and Colossians, two letters which Paul wrote about the same time. The letter to the church at Philippi is a more personal letter. In it, doctrine is interspersed with a conversational type of approach and style. In the light of this, the setting for the material in 2:19-30 is not unnatural.

Secondly, and more importantly, there *are* real links between these verses and earlier ones. These can be highlighted by associating 2:4 with 2:21 where consideration of the interests and needs of others is the common theme. Further, death is connected with such service as 2:8,17,30 make clear. Given these lines of continuity and the contrast to them which is subsequently presented in 3:2,18,19, the section which is now to be considered could not be more closely related to what precedes and what follows. It looks as if Paul, having emphasised the importance of the mind of Christ between church members, proceeds to illustrate the same with reference to gospel workers and churches. The mind of Christ is an essential for those in the Christian ministry.

We will consider this section in the light of that line of thought and focus particularly on what is said first about Timothy and then, Epaphroditus. But before we look at what is said about each man, we should consider what is common to both. From verses 19,23,25 and 28, it can be seen that this consists in their being sent.

Though the verb which Paul uses in all these verses is the general term for **to send** (*pempo*) and not the more official word, *apostello*, which gives us our term *apostle*, we need to note that Paul describes Epaphroditus as an *apostolos* (verse 25, translated messenger). We may therefore deduce that anyone who was sent by another *could* be described as an *apostolos* e.g. Timothy. Both verbs are used with reference to Jesus Christ and his having been sent by his Father and the noun *apostolos* is also used of him (Hebrews 3:1).

This raises two questions. First, what is the status of those apostles referred to in the New Testament who did not belong to the group of twelve chosen by Jesus personally (cf. Acts

14:14; Romans 16:7; 2 Corinthians 8:23)? Secondly, and by extension, are there or can there be apostles in the church today; and if so, of what kind are they?

Clearly, the New Testament informs us that in the period covered by Acts to Revelation there were other apostles in the churches besides those called by Jesus during his earthly ministry. But this does not mean that all apostles were of the same kind. The differences can be summarised in the following way.

While all apostles were sent, not all had the same sender, the same mission or the same endowment. There were those who were chosen, sent personally by the Lord Jesus Christ and with his authority. Before Christ's death, they included Judas Iscariot; after the resurrection, they included Matthias (cf. Acts 1:15 ff.) and Paul. The latter had seen him physically after his resurrection and been given his words by the Spirit of truth. But there were others who were chosen by the churches in obedience to the leading of the Spirit (Acts 13:1-3) and sent to carry the gospel to the unbelieving world, or to bear gifts, or some other church designated task. Barnabas was an example of the first (so was Paul as well) and Epaphroditus of the second but hard distinctions should not be drawn between roles within this second category.

The designation *apostle* could, therefore, be applied to two groups of people in the churches, namely, to apostles of Christ and also to apostles of the churches. The first have no successors, Paul himself was the last. They were all male. The second will continue in the church until the return of Christ and can perhaps include females (Romans 16:7), since there is some uncertainty as to whether the second name was Junias or Junia. Coming into this second category, there have been, from time to time throughout the history of the church, those whose outstanding zeal and usefulness, usually found in a time of decline or of breaking new ground, have merited the adjective *apostolic* or in a looser sense the noun *apostle*. Of course this was recognised by others and not by themselves. But whether that is done or not, and we think it better if it is not, as a regular practice, nothing must be allowed to cancel out the uniqueness of the first group in our thinking. They stand alone as those who laid the doctrinal foundation of Christ's church for all time. They alone were appointed personally by Jesus Christ.

All who are sent by Christ personally, or by the church, are connected with the Father's sending of his Son into the world. The Lord Jesus said, 'As the Father has sent me, I am sending you' (John 20:21). In the verses being considered this is brought out by the expressions **the work of the gospel** in verse 22 and **the work of Christ** in verse 30. Paul, the apostle of Jesus Christ, Timothy, his helper and Epaphroditus, the minister of the church at Philippi are all engaged in this one work. It is not only to be thought of in terms of the gospel message of salvation from sin and its consequences but every aspect of their pastoral work including concern for the churches (2 Corinthians 11:28). This would include their planning, journeys, absence from and return to churches. All these were to be done **in the Lord** (verses 19,24,29), for he was the one to whose will they deferred and the one on whom they depended for the accomplishment of their intentions. They were but servants. This is stated explicitly in verse 22 with reference to Paul and Timothy but surely applied to Epaphroditus as well.

Timothy (verses 19-24)

What Paul says about Timothy can be viewed in terms of the father-son relationship which existed between them (verse 22). This has a twofold significance.

First, it points to the strong likelihood that Timothy had become a Christian through the ministry of the apostle Paul. In 1 Timothy 1:2 (cf. 1 Corinthians 4:17), Paul describes him as his *true son in the faith*. When Paul revisited Lystra on his second missionary journey, Timothy was an established disciple (Acts 16:1). Probably, Timothy had heard Paul preaching in Lystra, his hometown, and witnessed the sufferings for the faith which the apostle had endured (Acts 14:19). By such means, the influence and instruction of Timothy's mother and grandmother (2 Timothy 1:5; 3:15) came to its desired fruition under the good hand of God.

Secondly, and this is what is in view in the section being considered, there was a co-operation between them in the cause of the Lord. Timothy was well thought of by Christian people in Lystra and Iconium when Paul returned there. After choosing Silas to replace Barnabas, Paul also resolved to take Timothy with them, probably as a result of prophetic announcements that the Lord had chosen him for his service (1 Timothy 1:18). Timothy was, therefore, with Paul at Philippi and the church there was impressed with his genuineness and worth.

His spiritual calibre had also been demonstrated to Paul in the course of their serving together. This was because of the loving respect which Timothy showed to Paul and his willingness to learn from him. As a result, Paul's love and respect for Timothy increased and though the one was an apostle of Jesus Christ and the other was not, the one who was not did not serve *under* but **with** the one who was (verse 22).

The mind of Christ which was possessed by Paul was also in Timothy and it prevailed between them.

Paul was sure, therefore, that even if he were not released and could not go to Philippi, Timothy would truly represent him among them and, what is more, represent Jesus Christ as well. He would put them before himself and care for them (verses 20,21). That was not true of all who were involved in Christ's work (verse 21 cf. 1:15,17). Though Paul valued having Timothy with him, he would not keep him one moment longer than was absolutely necessary. He would not put his own well being and joy before that of the Philippians (verse 23). Such thinking reveals the mind of Christ.

Epaphroditus (verses 25-29)
My brother (verse 25) is the first thing which Paul says about Epaphroditus. This description provides a perspective for considering everything else which is recorded about him. When one realises that Epaphroditus was a Gentile and remembers that Paul was a Jew, that description points to the reality of God's transforming grace on the level of human animosity. As verse 22 makes use of the father/son relationship we have a clear indication of how the gospel enobles further what is best in human relationships.

The name Epaphroditus, which means *handsome/comely*, was derived from Aphrodite, the Greek Venus, the goddess of love and beauty. Doubtless, he was a convert to Christ from idolatry and, as a result, a new and true beauty pervaded his character. The name he bore was not uncommon in Greek society and it had a contracted form which was Epaphras (Philemon 23; Colossians 1:7; 4:12). Most probably these were not one and the same person, though that is open to argument.

Epaphroditus brought the Philippians' gift to Paul and, in all probability, was entrusted with Paul's letter by way of response. Paul is anxious that the church should regard Epaphroditus no less highly than Timothy and that both should be received with equal affection and respect (cf. verse 29). He, therefore, gives them some information about Epaphroditus and how faithfully he had discharged his responsibility. This was perhaps to prevent any misunderstanding as to why Timothy was being kept back for a while but Epaphroditus was returning to them. His return is explained by two facts, namely, his longing for the Philippians and his concern about the effect which the news of his illness would have had on them (verse 26). This thoughtfulness of others is the mind of Christ at work once more.

Perhaps Paul and Epaphroditus had never actually met before but it is clear that they discovered a kindred spirit in each other, becoming close colleagues and comrades in arms (verse 25). In prison, they worked shoulder to shoulder and fought back to back in the cause of Christ, even when facing the reality of death. Epaphroditus was no mere postman, handing over a gift, but, at great cost to himself, a faithful minister on behalf of the church to Paul's total need. The mind of Christ is seen here in their serving each other's interests.

For Paul, therefore, to have been deprived of the fellowship of Epaphroditus through his death would have been a heavy burden to bear, even though his beloved Timothy was with him. It would have added an extra cause of sorrow to what was already being experienced due to his imprisonment and afflictions. To send him back to the Philippians was not easy either, though it would bring gladness to them. Paul would miss him but the joy of the Philippians and Epaphro-

ditus at being together again outweighed all personal considerations. It would also be one sorrow less. The mind of Christ
is seen at work once more, putting the joy of others before
one's own.

The serious illness of Epaphroditus and his being delivered from death exemplifies important truths for the whole
healing debate. First of all, good health is not always the
purpose of God for his servants and sickness is not always the
consequence of sin. (The same is true regarding wealth, see
4:11ff. and comment). Secondly, it is significant that it is
deliverance from imminent death and restoration to health
which is implied in these verses. This is more than a temporary alleviation of symptoms. Thirdly, all the emphasis is on
the **mercy** of God, which is his pity at the plight of the needy.
That is the ultimate explanation of any healing and not the
exercise of a gift possessed or the constraint imposed by the
existence of sufficient faith in the sufferer. While mercy is
sovereign, God is often pleased to work in extremities,
doubtless in answer to the supplication of his people.

7. *PERSONAL TESTIMONY STATED: (3:1-14)*

It has often been pointed out that the apostle's tone changes
in the opening verses of this chapter. Because of that and
other factors some have argued that the bulk of this chapter
belongs to another letter which he wrote to the Philippians.

The support which is presented for such an idea is that the
words used in the first part of verse 1, prior to the change of
tone, recur in 4:1,4. The intervening section is, therefore,
deduced to be not part of the original letter. In addition, the
word **Finally** in 3:1 is regarded as indicating that the letter
was about to be concluded. By the same reasoning, 4:10-20

is regarded by some as yet another letter because the word *Finally* is used in 4:8. The result of this thinking is that the epistle as we have it is not a single letter but an amalgamation of three.

There are good reasons for disregarding this notion. First, it is entirely hypothetical. No manuscript evidence exists for it at all. Secondly, a better explanation can be given for the text as it stands in chapter 3 than can be presented for the suggested amalgamation. This alternative explanation demonstrates the connections between various parts of the epistle and therefore its literary integrity.

First, the change of tone is not as abrupt as has been argued because Paul has already referred to the reality of conflict, the existence and activity of adversaries and called on the Philippians to make an appropriate response to their attacks (1:27,28). The strong exhortation in 3:2 is, therefore, not something which is wholly unexpected. Secondly, the affectionate address still continues with the words **my brothers**. Paul records his previously given oral warning because of a loving desire for the Philippians' safety. Thirdly, the warning in verse 2 is prefaced by a command to **rejoice in the Lord** and joy is one of the recurring themes, scattered throughout the letter. It is not cancelled out by the stern warning. Then, the term **Finally** should not be understood literalistically here (or in 4:8) as indicating a conclusion, nor should it be regarded as meaning nothing at all, as some have facetiously argued by analogy with its use in some sermons! It has a kind of metaphorical meaning e.g. *furthermore* and serves to underline something which is to be emphasised (cf. 1 Corinthians 7:29 where NIV has *What I mean*). A kind of summary is made of what has been said. We proceed, then, on the basis of the original unity of the letter as we have it.

There are two exhortations in the opening verses of this chapter and it is important that they should be associated with each other. They bracket together joy and a carefulness which is conducive to safety. The Philippians are not to rejoice as if there were no danger. Happiness in the Lord is not blind to the existence of threatening error. The Philippians are neither to be glum nor innocents abroad.

In order that they might be both glad and safe, Paul resolves to write **the same things** to them. The things he has in mind are those which he goes on to write about in the verses which immediately follow. But the use of the adjective *same* raises the question *same as what*? The answer, of course, is the same as he had previously taught them while he was with them in person. Verse 18 contains a similar type of reference. These allusions raise an important point of doctrine, namely, the consistency of apostolic teaching not merely in what is actually written in Scripture but between what is recorded there and what was taught by word of mouth.

It does not need to be said that we do not have in Scripture all that the apostles taught. Paul refers in 2 Thessalonians 2:15 to the traditions which he handed on by word of mouth or by letter. But what we do have in writing is in perfect accord with, not in contradiction to, what was taught orally. Where a disagreement exists between what is written in Scripture and what *a church* claims to possess of unwritten apostolic traditions (as in the cases of Roman Catholicism and Eastern Orthodoxy) what is written in Scripture takes the primary position. There is urgent need today to give to Scripture its supreme position over human and church traditions - and that includes Protestantism as well as the religious communions just mentioned.

These words, which come at the end of verse 1, may give

a clue as to how this letter was actually composed. Paul might have entertained the thought of drawing his letter to a close with the opening words of verse 1, namely, **Rejoice in the Lord** only to be impressed by the Holy Spirit with the need to spell out once more the things which he had previously emphasised. Repetition is often beneficial.

Such a possibility is quite in keeping with Scripture being the word of God written under the inspiration of the Holy Spirit because the nature of that inspiration harmonises with the natural processes in the minds of the human writers. For a parallel we can think of Paul's sudden flights of exultation regarding Christ or the gospel; Jude's change of intention, as he contemplated writing his letter (Jude verse 3); and the writer of the epistle to the Hebrews who postponed a discussion of the significance of Melchizedek (5:10). Who has not wished that Paul had expanded on what he told the church at Thessalonica regarding the man of sin (2 Thessalonians 2:3, especially verses 6,7) but, on reflection, adored the divine wisdom that he did not do so. It is better not to know some things which we might very much like to know! However, whether Paul was the recipient of a sudden impulse of the Spirit at this point in Philippians or not, it is clear the Lord regarded the content of verses 2-20 as something that he wanted spelt out in Scripture. Though the importance of this passage is often acknowledged, the particular divine impetus which lay behind it has not always been recognised.

Verses 2-14
Though we have argued that the warning expressed in verse 2 is not unheralded, its strength and severity remain to be considered. Three features disclose the intensity of the apostle's feeling on this matter. First, he uses the imperative

watch out for three times in this verse and not once as in the NIV. From a grammatical point of view, the first use would have been sufficient to connect what immediately follows but the repetition indicates how concerned the apostle was to rouse the Philippians and to put them on red alert with regard to this danger. Secondly, those who are presenting the threat are described not once but three times, from different angles and in exceedingly emotive language. Clearly, Paul does not want the Philippians to fail to see these foes for what they really are. Thirdly, he uses a biting sarcasm as in various ways he shows how empty their boasting is.

A discussion of the identity of these opponents of the Christian cause, referred to in this letter, is now unavoidable. So far we have been able to consider the material in 1:15-17,28,29; 2:14-16 without referring to this question. But with the more detailed statements of 3:2,18,19 and the heavily loaded inferences in verses 3:12-16, this difficult and controverted problem area has to be treated.

In our view, the procedure which is adopted with regard to this matter is crucial. It is a mistake to gather all these verses together on the assumption that they all describe a single enemy. Rather, each piece of information has to be considered by itself to see what it actually says and then, on the basis of the results of such a study, a decision can be reached as to what kind of foe is being described. Whether a single enemy is in view or not can then be determined in the light of all the evidence. We offer the following summary of our position which favours the view that several dangerous trends are being highlighted.

As 1:15-17 refers to brothers who preach Christ, these persons must be regarded as Christians who make known the same gospel as Paul preached. The fault with which they are charged is in the realm of their motivation and not their message or even emphasis. This accords with what Paul writes in 2:20-22. Such people as these cannot in any sense be described as adversaries of the gospel cause like those in 1:28 who are exposed to destruction. Such Christian brothers, therefore, form a grouping on their own. They are not wholly in the right but they are certainly not wholly in the wrong.

In 2:15, as we have seen, the description given relates to the general moral condition of Philippian society. It is possible that this can be associated with what is said in 1:28 on the basis that the crooked and depraved are likely to oppose Christians and their message.

But what of the several pieces of information in chapter 3? Verse 2 has an unmistakeable Jewish dimension. The evidence for that is plain and compelling. The use of the word for **circumcision** in verse 3, which sets up a telling contrast with the word in verse 2 translated **mutilators**, settles that matter. Unabated and inveterate opposition to the Christian cause did come from the Jewish quarter. It is, therefore, possible that the opponents mentioned in 1:28 included Jews and not only Gentiles.

But were these Jews unbelievers or Judaizers? This is the big question. The latter were Jews who, though they had professed faith in Jesus as the Messiah, not only persisted in observing Jewish practices themselves but required Gentile believers to observe them too as being essential for salvation. It has to be admitted that either identification is possible in terms of what verse 2 actually says. In addition, the narratives in Acts and the situation addressed in Galatians bear out the existence of threats from each quarter. The choice is not easy to make. We prefer on balance to regard these as Judaizers but insist that they are not to be identified with those referred to in 1:14 because Judaizers are called *false brothers* by Paul in his letter to the Galatians and not *brothers*.

The content of 3;18,19 may help a little at this juncture if what is said in it indicates that those referred to had made some kind of Christian profession. If they had, then it *is* Judaizers who are in view and not unbelievers. But there is once more a lack of agreement on this point. In our view, the language which the apostle used can be satisfactorily understood without referring to a profession of faith having been made. It describes a way of life which is not only opposed to that of the apostle and others like him, but also to the purpose which Christ had in dying, namely, to redeem from the guilt of sin and a life of sinning. One does not have to think of a contradiction between lip and life, so to speak, in order to do justice to these terms. 3:18 and 19, therefore, could refer to unbelievers.

The option we adopt, therefore, is to see the references in the early part of the chapter as referring to Judaizers and those at the end of the chapter to free-thinking, free-living Gentiles. The references to perfection in the middle of the chapter can be understood as referring to all who understood perfection as attainable in ways other than through Christ, whether Jew or Gentile. They are amenable to either identification.

Verses 2 and 3 should be considered in close association with each other because each verse provides one half of the great contrast which they together express. Two groups of people are in view. The first (verse 2) comprises those whose religious understanding was first and foremost, Jewish. These would include not only native Jews but also proselytes. These are the Judaizers (or unbelieving Jews). Christian people comprised the second (verse 3) that is, not only

Gentiles, but Jews, whether native or proselyte, who had come to believe in Jesus.

Having identified the two groups which are contrasted in these verses, we must now try to gauge the dimensions of the contrast actually depicted. It is the expression which begins verse 3 which points up the contrast most precisely and that in two respects.

First of all, the pronoun **we** which is located at the beginning of the original text is emphatic. Its significance is well brought out in the NIV rendering **For it is we who**. The contrast is, therefore, to be understood in terms of those in the second group being what those in the first group were not.

This has relevance to the pluralism of the multi-faith outlook of the present time. As it is Judaism and Christianity which are being set over against each other, in spite of the fact that they have the Old Testament in common, it is surely not possible to bracket Christianity with *other* religions. From this it follows that Jews, in the religious sense, and Christians are not together the people of God and so Christians and adherents of other faiths do not belong together in that way either. All religions do not somehow ultimately cohere and all who are religious cannot somehow be gathered together into one community.

But to appreciate the full significance of the contrast in verses 2 and 3 we must note that Paul records **we who are the circumcision** with reference to Christians. That is staggering reversal. How could Paul, who was a native Jew, make such an astounding declaration?

By saying that it was Christians who were the circumcision, Paul meant to make clear that they possessed what circumcision represented. Circumcision was a seal to Abraham of God's covenant with him and also a sign to others that he belonged to it. But it did not only have an individual reference. All his male descendants were to bear that mark in their bodies (Genesis 17:9-14). The sign of circumcision showed that God was laying claim to a people.

But many in the nation lacked the faith of Abraham, though they were circumcised and traced their lineage to him (John 8:33-47). They were, therefore, called upon to circumcise their hearts (Deuteronomy 10:16; Jeremiah 4:4) and were described as uncircumcised along with the surrounding nations (Jeremiah 9:25-26). Stephen summarised the history of the nation in these terms (Acts 7:51). So, in the Old Testament period, to be circumcised in the flesh did not always mean that circumcision of the heart had taken place (though that is what it represented). Such were not the people of God, as Paul teaches in Romans 2:28,29. By contrast, all who are Christians have been circumcised in heart (Colossians 2:11,12).

To be without this inward circumcision/purification, after the Messiah has come, is to have only a concision (mutilation). The self-inflicted lacerations of Israel's pagan neighbours, which Israel was forbidden to copy, may very well be in Paul's mind at this point because the Greek term which he coins comes from the Greek translation of Leviticus 21:5 which refers to a cutting which God had forbidden. In Galatians 5:12 his language becomes even more vehement - such is the importance of the matter being dealt with as is shown in Galatians 6:12-16.

As Jews who have not believed in Christ are outside the new covenant they are described as **dogs** and **men who do evil**. Dogs were detestable animals to Jews and their forbears. They were regarded as carrying impurity and causing injury. To call someone a dog was an expression of disdain and worthlessness (1 Samuel 17:43; 2 Samuel 16:9). It could also express religious and moral contempt as in Deuteronomy 23:18 where it is used of male temple prostitutes. When Jesus used the term he employed it only in a religious or moral sense (Matthew 7:6;15:26) unlike the Jews who also conveyed a detestation of people by means of it. But here Paul uses the term of opprobrium with regard to *the Jews* in order to express the fact that they did not have the approval of God which they thought they possessed.

Something similar exists with reference to the next description, *men who do evil.* In the Psalter, David complains to God about evil workers and the way in which they opposed and even persecuted the righteous, for example, in Psalms 5:5 and 6:8 etc. But here Paul regards the pro-Jewish party as the wicked and, by implication, the Christians as the righteous. In 2 Corinthians 11:13 he describes the Judaizers as deceitful workers.

In view of the strength of these denunciations it may perhaps be important to make clear that Paul is not declaring that there is no salvation for Jews, nor that there is no future for the Jewish people in the saving purpose of God. Romans 11 deals with these points but it also makes clear that such salvation comes about by means of the proclamation of the gospel and not a reintroduction of the old covenant and speaks of a time when Israel, almost as a whole, will come into the international church of Christ.

What it means to be circumcised in Christ by a divine surgery is set out in the remainder of verse 3. Three activities are listed which contrast with the merely physical sign. We consider each in turn.

First, Christians **worship by the Spirit of God**. The statement points to much more than the sincere/formal disjunction with regard to worship. It is the Spirit of God who is referred to and not the spirit of a believer, though a true sincerity is the kind of worshipping which is necessarily involved. The Spirit's activity is the consequence of the glorification of Jesus Christ by his death and resurrection (John 7:38,39). As such, Christians not only worship in a way which is very different from the formal observance of the Levitical requirements but with far greater understanding and liberty than that of Old Testament saints. Christians come boldly to God (cf. 1:2 and what is said there regarding God as Father and what is said about courage in 1:20).

Secondly, they **glory in Christ Jesus**. Here the contrast becomes a little more explicit with the use of the verb for *glory* or *boast*. The covenant of blessing which was graciously made with the children of Israel should have been responded to by them with humble awe and gratitude. Instead, lacking faith, their hearts were lifted up (Deuteronomy 8:14) in spite of being warned against such boasting (Jeremiah 9:23-24). Christians boast in Jesus Christ in whom all the promised blessings exist. This is to be expanded in verses 7-11.

The third aspect, **who put no confidence in the flesh**, may be understood as the negative corollary of the second. To boast and to trust are closely connected because one boasts in what one trusts has merit or brings one gain. Jesus Christ and the flesh are therefore opposites in this context and that gives a clue to the meaning of *flesh* in this verse. It obviously includes circumcision (cf. Galatians 6:12-15) but in the light of the verses which follow it must include more and stand for all that is personal as distinct from what belongs to Jesus Christ.

Verse 4 is a kind of bridging statement, relating both to

what precedes and what follows. The first part serves to prove that Paul had not been speaking ignorantly about Jewish privileges which he had disregarded. He declares that he could have boasted in such things as well, had he a mind to do so. (In the past he most certainly had!) In the second part he goes even further, to assert that as far as such privileges were concerned, he had more than many of his fellow nationals. He then proceeds to list what these were.

Why does he do that? It is distinctly possible that an attempt was being made by his detractors to discredit his message and ministry in the estimate of the Philippians by trying to gain an advantage of him on this matter. Something like that had happened at Corinth (cf. 2 Corinthians 10-14) and in Galatia. In both he defended the validity of his apostolic credentials. Here in Philippians he deals with the same kind of charge by speaking about salvation and the Lord Jesus Christ.

In verses 5 and 6 Paul lists seven distinctive grounds which he had for boasting. The first four relate to his physical descent, which can be described as having come to him by divine providence, while the remaining three were the result of effort and achievement on his part.

With reference to his birth, parentage and upbringing (verse 5a) Paul makes it clear that he was a Jew with a rich pedigree. He had been **circumcised on the eighth day**, the very day specified in the Old Testament (Genesis 17:12; Leviticus 12:3), and not later like Ishmael or a pagan convert. That implies something about his parents' belief. **Israel** was the dignified name for the people of God and Paul came from such stock. He belonged to **the tribe of Benjamin** and that counted for something too. There was much that was illustrious about the tribe of Benjamin in spite of its numerical smallness (Psalm 68:27) and the blemishes in its history (cf. Judges 19-21). Paul regarded his tribal connection as a matter of importance (Romans 11:1).

Benjamin was the son of Jacob's favourite wife, Rachel, and was his only son to be born in the land of promise (Genesis 35:16-18). Israel's first king was a Benjaminite (1 Samuel 9:1,2). Was Paul named after King Saul? The tribe remained loyal to the Davidic dynasty after the division of the kingdom (1 Kings 12:21) and the city of Jerusalem and the temple lay within its territory (Judges 1:21). It had a position of honour when the army of Israel was drawn up in battle array.

The use of the term **a Hebrew of the Hebrews** in what follows points to more than the racial identity of Paul and his parents. It refers to the language in which they were fluent. Many Jews lived outside Palestine in New Testament times and were only able to speak Greek. Though Paul was born to Jews who lived in Tarsus, they and he were able to speak Hebrew and that included Aramaic (cf. Acts 21:40; 22:2; 26:14). Paul was taught Hebrew at home and sent by his parents to Jerusalem as a young boy (Acts 22:3). He was a Hebrew Jew and not a Hellenistic one (Acts 6:1).

Moving on from such a notable pedigree and upbringing, Paul lists his personal achievements in relation to the law. He does this by identifying himself as a Pharisee and referring to his **zeal** and to his **righteousness** (verse 5b).

First of all, he declares that he was **a Pharisee**. He had been taught by Gamaliel, the leading Pharisee of his day (Acts 22:3; 5:34). This was doubtless because his father or his forbears were Pharisees (Acts 23:6). According to Paul, this party was 'the strictest sect of (our) religion' (Acts 26:5). They were the party of law. Their designation was derived from an Aramaic word which means *to be separate*, that is, from all that was prohibited in the law, together with the traditions which had been allegedly deduced from it (cf. Mark 7:1-19). The Pharisees would have described Judaism in terms of the whole of a person's life being submitted to all the requirements of the law and they would have looked back to the time of Ezra for their origin. The synagogue was the focal point of their religion in contrast to their religious disputants, the Sadducees, who were a priestly and pro-temple party.

Secondly, what Paul proceeds to say about his zeal and his righteousness are manifestations of the intensity and sincerity of his commitment to uphold the law at all costs. His zeal was shown by his opposition to the Christian church; his righteousness by adherence to his own religion.

While Paul does not specify in verse 6 that his zeal was related to the upholding of the law and its associated traditions, that may be safely assumed. He spells it out elsewhere, namely, Acts 22:3-5 and Galatians 1:14. He was indeed a zealot, sparing himself no hardship and showing no mercy to the church which lived by another rule (Galatians 6:16; Acts 26:9-11). In all of that he would have been convinced that he was offering a service to God (John 16:2).

The bottom line of his confidence before God was related to his being faultless in the light of the law. This was his righteousness and, given the innumerable requirements that were made of him, it was no small attainment. The prayer of the Pharisee in the parable which Jesus told, together with the answer of the rich young ruler to Jesus' question, give an accurate picture of what Paul is referring to at this point (Luke 18:11,12,21). To be blameless does not amount to a claim to be sinless but rather to an honest belief that no conscious fault has been committed.

In verses 7-14 we have Paul's testimony as a Christian and though he speaks autobiographically elsewhere in the New Testament, this is a unique passage.

In Acts and the Epistles he records the factual details of his conversion and call, acknowledging God's great mercy to him in Jesus Christ (Acts 22:6-16; 26:12-18; Romans 1:5; Galatians 1:15; Ephesians 3:2ff; Colossians 1:23, 25 and 1 Timothy 1:12-17). In the passage before us, however, he speaks about all this from within and describes the change of mind which he experienced.

In an age when spiritual experience is so sought after, cultivated and, sad to say, manufactured, a passage like this will supply much needed clarification, correction and direction. It will expose the false and also the superficial but maintain the great importance of the experiential in the Christian life. These verses unpack what Paul meant in 1:21 by the words, *For to me, to live is Christ and to die is gain.*

We begin with the verb which Paul uses once in verse 7 and twice in verse 8 which the NIV translates as **consider**. Two points need to be made about it. First, we need to recall that Paul has used this verb before - in three contexts which are very important for the overall message of this letter. These are 2:3,6,25. It is 2:6 which provides the foundational and dominant thought, namely, how the pre-existent Christ thought about his deity. This supplies an index for how Christians are to think and act towards each other (2:3) and how ministers of Christ are to consider and conduct themselves towards the flock. While the verb necessarily involves a mental process, it is not theoretical and unproductive in terms of action.

Secondly, Paul employs this verb in different tenses in verses 7 and 8. In verse 7, it is the perfect tense which he uses and this refers to a completed act in the past, the effects of which continue. The present tense is used in verse 8, twice, to indicate his state of mind at the time of writing this letter. Verse 7 refers to the Damascus road; verse 8 to the Roman prison. Some thirty years had elapsed between the two. It would, therefore, have been much better if the NIV had not used the present tense in verse 7.

Though Paul makes clear in verses 4-6 that he had no lack of Jewish privileges and attainments in which he could have boasted had he wished to do so, we would not be wrong to think of him as having done so for much of his life. Why did he cease doing so? What brought about that great change? The answer is supplied in verse 7.

Profit and **loss** are opposites. No businessman mistakes either for the other. Furthermore, every businessman wants to turn his losses into gains and to prevent his gains from becoming losses. As Saul of Tarsus, Paul knew what his gains were and what was loss. The former was bound up with his being a Jew and a Pharisee and the latter, with being a Christian. That was how he would have set out his spiritual balance sheet - until he met Jesus the Lord (Jehovah) on the road to Damascus. It was then that he saw all his gains to be in reality losses, because they did not include Christ; and what had seemed total and utter loss, to be immeasurable gain. So, for the sake of Christ, he parted with what he had held dear and embraced what he had previously despised. Like the merchant seeking goodly pearls, he parted gladly with all he had previously gathered in order to buy one pearl whose worth exceeded all that he had (Matthew 13:45, 46).

But Paul was not content to repeat a thirty year old testimony, as many might be. He wanted to say something up to date about what Jesus Christ meant to him. Verses 8-11 comprise that statement. It is probably the most fervent outpouring of devotion to Christ recorded in Holy Scripture and is made up of a declaration of his present feelings (verse 8) and of his desires for the future (verses 9-11). Then, in verses 12-16, Paul records a determination to pursue the fulfilment of his desire.

His Devotion (verse 8)

This is expressed in the whole of verse 8, apart from the very last words. Its opening words are untranslateable as they stand but the NIV's rendering **What is more** brings out their force very well because Paul is not only endorsing what he has just said but exceeding it. This can be proved from a comparison of verse 8 with verse 7 which shows that, in addition to the change of tense of the verb which has been noted, the following intensifications of thought must be highlighted. They are:

1. From the things that were **profit** to **everything**
2. From **loss** to **rubbish**
3. From **Christ** to **Christ Jesus my Lord**. This last expression is not found anywhere else in the New Testament and provides the explanation for all the other changes.

These words make two things clear about the interval between his conversion and the writing of this epistle. First, he had entertained no second thoughts about the transaction which he had made on the Damascus road. Secondly, not only were Paul's Jewish credentials still *loss*, they had become **rubbish** and so had everything else too e.g. Roman citizenship, a classical education etc.- anything which could have stood to his credit. The word which the NIV renders as *rubbish* includes the meaning of scraps of rotting food which would be given to dogs (verse 2) or even dung. It expresses, therefore, the strongest revulsion and rejection when compared with the pricelessness and peerlessness of Jesus Christ.

Paul's realisation of the preciousness of Jesus Christ grew by means of **knowing** him. Knowledge, whether intellectual or mystical, was highly prized in the Gentile world as is made clear by the letters to the church at Corinth. Paul, however, is thinking of knowledge as a Hebrew would and that means that it was not getting something, but gaining someone. *To know* in Hebrew is a way of describing a relationship with someone, which can, and should, be a most enriching experience. But as it is a personal relationship with *Jesus*, in all the great enrichment of his characteristics and capacities, which is in view, every other relationship is surpassed. Compared with it, every loss is no loss at all and every gain is rubbish.

His Desire (verses 8-10)

Paul expresses his desire in verses 8-10 by means of four verbs. They are to **gain**, to **be found in**, to **know**, and to **attain**. Three of these most probably refer to what he expects on the last day - the day of Christ. The other, to **know**, the third mentioned above, obviously relates to something ongoing and increasing in this life. The correlating of these two horizons of expectation, the temporal and the eternal, indicates that a desire to be with Christ in heaven must be accompanied by a desire to be with and for him on earth for it to be genuine and for it ultimately to be fulfilled.

We focus on the second verb, namely, **be found in** (verse 9). Paul has already used this verb in 2:8 with reference to the incarnate Christ. There it perhaps means no more than actually being human. The same meaning could hold good for this verse. If so, it means that Paul desired to be always in Christ. But perhaps what Paul actually had in mind was his being found in Christ when he was subjected to the divine scrutiny on the last day. Whichever is the case, and we prefer the latter, central to the matter is what he goes on to say about righteousness. There is no way in which anyone can be in Christ, either on earth or in heaven, for time and eternity, except by righteousness. No one can be saved if righteousness is waived. But whose righteousness saves?

Two kinds of righteousness are spoken of in verse 9. They are not only differentiated but contrasted. They are described in terms of their origins and, by implication, their effects. As one of these is definitely rejected, they are not capable of being amalgamated in any way.

The first kind Paul describes as **a righteousness of my own that comes from the law**. This is the kind which Paul had (verse 6) but which he came to reject. The reason for his rejection of it is implied by its connection in the verse with his desire to be found in Christ, that is, this righteousness would not avail for that purpose. This was because it was his own which came from the law.

The possessive adjective *my* is emphatic and so the translation **my own** is required in order to distinguish this righteousness from anyone else's and to describe its quality as something which is peculiarly Paul's.

The other words **from the law** reinforce this and disclose how Paul came by this righteousness. He got it by dealing with the law, that is, by doing what the law required. It was, therefore, by his works of obedience and was something in which he could boast (verses 4b-6). It was a self-righteousness - a righteousness in himself. The inescapable conclusion from this is that if anyone is to be found in Christ it must be by a righteousness which belongs to someone else and not oneself (cf. Ephesians 2:9).

Paul proceeds to describe this alternative righteousness. First, he records that it is **through faith in Christ**. Though Paul will go on to speak about the relationship between this righteousness and God, the fact that he begins by speaking of Christ is consistent with the Christ-centredness of this passage of devotional writing and the fact that God is only known savingly in Jesus Christ. Paul learned that on the road to Damascus.

There is some debate about the NIV translation at this point and it has to be admitted that the Greek could be rendered *the faith of Christ*. In support of the NIV translation is the fact that Paul does not speak elsewhere of Christ's faith in relation to righteousness but of his obedience. Against it is the fact that, whenever in the New Testament, the noun *faith* is followed by a reference to someone it is that person's faith which is being referred to and not faith in that person. Many scholars prefer to read *the faith of Christ* which carries the meaning that righteousness comes via Christ's own faith(fulness).

More important, however, than debating the question of which translation is better, is determining how *the faith of Christ* is to be understood. The danger is that it is simply thought of in subjective terms as trust in God which can mean very little. Christ's faith must be related to his obedience; his trusting was inseparably joined to doing and dying (1 Peter 2:23,24 and, of course, Philippians 2:8). This is in keeping with Paul's teaching about saving righteousness elsewhere (Romans 3:24,25; 5:17,19). It is via a death and not only a life.

This righteousness which is related to Christ is through him but it comes from God. He is its source. Its character is therefore divine and perfect - **from God** contrasts with **from**

the law earlier in the verse. This contrast must be carefully understood. The righteousness which comes from God is not other than or less than the righteousness which the law expresses and requires. It is one and the same because the law is the law of God. **From God** means that he provides the sinner with the righteousness which his law requires. He does so, however, on the basis of what Christ has done by way of obedience and not what sinners are required, and may try, to do (Romans 3:19-22).

The all important righteousness is therefore linked both to Christ and to God in the way described. But what about the twofold reference to faith in this verse? In particular, if we adopt the NIV translation **faith in Christ** in its earlier part do not the final words of verse 9 become redundant? We may be sure that the Bible does not contain anything superfluous which we may skip over.

The words **by faith** which come at the end of the verse are linked with the expression **from God**. They emphasise that God, who provides righteousness through Christ's life and death, determines that faith shall be the appropriate response or means of reception. Faith is not merely to appropriate what Christ has achieved but to also appropriate what God makes available.

Verse 9 is a definitive statement on the great doctrine of *Justification by faith alone* which relates to the conscious beginnings of the Christian life. Its inclusion at this point, in what is the expressed desire of someone who was a believer, and of whom it was therefore already true, demonstrates how foundational and influential it is for the ongoing and increasing *life* of a Christian. This is because it is by faith in Christ that anyone and every one comes into the relationship of being *in Christ* - a great emphasis of Paul's. Consequently,

Paul's desire exceeds being accepted by God through Christ. It extends to being conformed to Christ (cf. **becoming like him** in verse 10) and that increasingly this side of death and ultimately beyond it (verse 11).

Three clauses in verse 10 indicate what is involved in knowing or becoming like Christ, this side of death. The relationship between those clauses we understand in the following ways. The first two, that is, **the power of his resurrection** and **the fellowship of his sufferings** are to be correlated. They are the two parts of but a single whole. They can be distinguished but are not to be separated, either chronologically or as two stages in experience. The third clause describes the process (**becoming like him** is a present participle) by which the participation in the power of his resurrection and the fellowship of his sufferings takes place. We now proceed to examine Paul's statement on this basis.

The Christ whom Paul desired to know is the one who suffered, died and rose again. His devotion is not, therefore, a flight of fancy or a baseless mysticism. It has a foundation in reality, being directed towards one who had a space-time, flesh and blood history. But it is more than an acknowledgement of events or even a recollection of them. It is a living communion with that one who suffered, died and rose again. It is rooted in time and space but not limited to time and space, because it is focused on one who transcends the time and space which he created. This is the spiritual world - Christ in you the hope of glory (Colossians 1:27) - a blessed reality to all except those who think that this physical world is the only reality which exists.

It is surprising that Paul mentions resurrection first and secondly that he brackets it with sufferings and not with death. Why did he do this? The explanation we propose for the variation from the more usual pattern of death-resurrection, is along lines found in 1:19,20. There the Spirit's supply is seen as the fortifying preparation of Paul for whatever might lie ahead. In an identical way, the power of the resurrection not only enables the sufferer to cope but even to rise above the sufferings which are to be endured. This power belongs to God and it is manifested in the resurrection of Jesus from the dead (Ephesians 1:19,20) but is also operative in believers. As it dealt with death, it can deal with every limitation and opposition. Similar thoughts are found in 2 Corinthians 4:7-11.

What about the term *sufferings* instead of *death*? Paul's choice of the plural noun means that he is thinking of more than the suffering of death alone. From the fact that he speaks of these as Christ's sufferings being shared in, they are certainly not those which were a punishment for sin which Jesus bore alone. Paul uses the term cross (cf. 3:18) or blood to refer to the suffering of Christ as a sacrifice for sin. What Paul has in view here are those sufferings which came to Christ in the course of his earthly ministry in a fallen world. Those adversities and afflictions are not entirely exhausted. He bequeathed them to his servants who serve him in their generations (Colossians 1:24; 1 Peter 2:20-24 and also Philippians 1:29).

Communion with Christ means union with him in his death. It is neither possible to experience Christ's power nor to suffer for him without experiencing death, time and time again. What kind of death is this? It is a death like Christ's own - a hard, demanding one; a death to self, a bearing of one's own cross, for Christ did not please himself but suffered for God's glory and the good of others (Romans 15:2-3). To know Christ and to refuse to die daily is not possible.

We come now to what is said in verse 11 about knowing Christ on the other side of death. Paul has made it clear that to die would bring him a gain beyond what is possible in this life viz. that of being with Christ (1:23). He has also spoken of the power of Christ's resurrection being experienced in this life (verse 10). What more exists? Much more. Apart from what is referred to in 3:20,21, the verse before us says something amazing.

To do that, Paul coins a word. To be exact, he strengthens a word he has already used, namely, the simple word for resurrection (verse 10). He adds an extra preposition to the *re* part of resurrection which, of course, means *again*. Resurrection is rising again. What Paul wrote was *rising again from*. This means that death will be totally left behind. He will be shot of it. His heels will be clear of what dogged his steps. He will have reached LIFE.

But, to be exact, what he says is **from the dead** and not *from death*. While the latter is included in the former, resurrection from the dead means the general resurrection at the end of time in the day of Christ. Paul, having died, will rise from among the dead. The expression attests the reality of the physical resurrection and should not be used as the main text for a doctrine of secret rapture.

But is this astounding confidence not somewhat dented by the words **and so, somehow**? A more literal rendering of the Greek at this point might even seem to express a doubt namely *if by any means I might* (KJV). But if Paul had been expressing a doubt about whether he would be raised, he would have been contradicting what he had previously written in 1:10,23. The Greek expression involved, *ei pos,* is used in Acts 27:12; Romans 1:10 and 11:14 to express a hope, the attainment of which was not within the power of the one hoping. This holds good here because Paul was not able to bring about the resurrection which he was sure would take place. If, however, this interpretation be deemed inadequate because it does not do justice to the element of doubt perceived to exist in these words, reference may be made to the fact that Paul did not know what lay between him and the resurrection. While he was sure that he would be raised, he was genuinely unsure of how he would die, or indeed whether he would die at all (cf. 1 Thessalonians 4:15).

His Determination (verses 12-14)

The test of the genuineness of a desire is not the intensity of the language which is used to express it but whether it is followed by determined, strenuous activity to bring it to fulfilment. In these verses, Paul declares that the one thing which he always has before him is the goal of knowing, of gaining, Christ fully. His life bore out those words. He was no spiritual sluggard (cf. Proverbs 24:30-34).

But in these verses Paul reiterates and expands on his desire as well as recording his determination. This is done for particular reasons which can be deduced from these verses and their context. First, we note that Paul was in earnest at this point. He not only wants to clarify what he meant but also to exclude what was quite foreign to his thinking. He speaks positively to explain; negatively, to refute - and he does each twice (verses 12,13).

Why did he do this? One answer is that he wanted the Philippians to think and live as he and others were doing. Perhaps there were differences within the church itself on this matter (verses 15-17). There probably were. But something else needs to be brought within the frame. There were those who were influencing the church in the wrong direction. The two groups already considered from this chapter (Judaizers in verse 2 and Gentile libertines in verses 18-19) have to be brought in at this point. Though we have identified them in different ways, both could be alluded to in these verses because each had a view that perfection was attainable in this life, albeit by its own route. In the first century there were Jews and Gentiles who thought that *they had arrived*. They have their successors today. Christians are not to be among them.

What about the assertions? The verb translated **press on** (verses 12,14) declares Paul's single yet all-embracing attitude with regard to the goal. He not only contemplates it; he strives towards it. He refuses to allow even the gains which he has made in the Christian race to hinder him from pursuing greater gain, the greatest gain of all. It is well known that Paul uses athletic imagery at this point, as he does elsewhere in his writings. The point which he is making here is that the prize is not awarded before the race is completed and it is awarded to all who finish the course. It is, therefore, only to be looked for after the tape and not before it.

He describes the prize not only in relation to himself but in relation to Jesus Christ, **that for which Christ Jesus took hold of me** (verse 12), and to God, **the prize for which God has called me heavenwards in Christ Jesus** (verse 14). In relation to Jesus Christ (verse 12) Paul sees it as something which he wants to **take hold of** either because Jesus took hold of him (the same verb is used) or because he wants to possess what Jesus took hold of him for on the road to Damascus. The NIV favours the latter interpretation and in view of the fact that the Greek words in question do not mean *because* in 4:10, where they are also used and translated *indeed*, we agree with the NIV rendering. This means that Paul will only be content when he possesses all that Jesus Christ has for him. He will not allow himself to be satisfied with, or diverted by, the ground he has already gained when there is more land to be possessed.

Paul describes the prize in relation to God in verse 14. He does so by associating it with God's call. What is this? Some have understood it as the summons which a victor in an athletic contest would receive to approach the judges, or even the emperor, to receive his prize. Against this not wholly unsuitable idea, is the fact that Paul uniformly speaks of the call of God as a summons to salvation. It comes through the gospel of Jesus Christ with his gracious power and is heard at the beginning of the race, so to speak, and not after its end (1 Thessalonians 2:12). This is how we understand it, as a call to partake of all the holy bliss of heaven everlastingly.

The picture we have, then, of the apostle is of someone who still feels the pressure of having been grasped by Christ (verse 12) and who still hears the echoes of God's voice (verse 13), which coincided on the road to Damascus. Consequently he spent the rest of his life on the road to heaven.

8. PERSONAL TESTIMONY APPLIED: (3:15-21)

It is in this section that the purpose of the testimony being given begins to surface. It was certainly not for self display or to excite admiration. It was recorded by Paul, inspired by the Spirit, that its spiritual principles might be brought to bear on the lives of the Philippians. Those principles are: devotion to Christ as a person, trust in his righteousness before God, and increasing conformity to him through a willingness to

suffer in his company and for his cause, with his help, until
glory dawns and full likeness to him is achieved. Christian
people ought, therefore, to take it to themselves in the same
way.

Paul wants the Philippians to live according to the example which he and others like him had supplied (verse 17). That
model life was one in keeping with the gospel (1:27). Others
were living in a very different way (3:18ff.). They did not
regard the cross of Christ, the centre of the gospel, in the way
in which Paul and his colleagues did. The secret of Christian
living is Christian thinking (verse 15a).

The verb which the NIV translates as **take such a view** is
one which Paul chose to use frequently in the letter (1:7; 2:2
[twice]; 3:19; 4:2; and 4:10 [twice]). The other use of it is
particularly important and has already been noticed. It is in
2:5 where the thinking of Jesus Christ himself is referred to.
Christians must think as Jesus did if they would live as he did.

Verses 15 and 16 are not easy to understand. There is a
difficulty in each of the three parts which comprise them. We
will consider them in turn.

The difficulty in the first part of verse 15 relates to the
meaning of the word translated **mature** in the NIV. It is from
the same word family as **perfect** in verse 12 and merely to
mention that will raise the question as to how one and the
same person could make the second statement so soon after
the first. Some resolve the apparent contradiction by suggest-
ing that Paul is being ironical in verse 15, adopting the claim
to perfection which others are making. Paul was not above
using an irony, which at times was biting, in order to bring
people to their senses (e.g. 1 Corinthians 4:8). But the fact
that he includes himself among the mature in verse 15
presents a difficulty for this interpretation.

It is, therefore, better to look for a different meaning in verse 15 from that stated in verse 12. Paul frequently used the adjective with the meaning of *adult* or *mature* (1 Corinthians 2:6;14:20; Ephesians 4:13; Colossians 1:28). That meaning would do nicely at this point. Behind the reference to personal maturity lies the thought of spiritual development, which includes a basic competence with regard to the use as well as the knowledge of divine things (Hebrews 5:13,14).

Paul calls upon the mature, then, to show their maturity by thinking as he did. Agreement with Paul's thought pattern becomes a test of maturity. The mature are those who know that the perfection which is complete likeness to Christ lies beyond this life and are not only confident about obtaining it, but intent on doing so.

With regard to the second part of verse 15 there are two difficulties. The first lies in identifying what Paul is referring to by **some point**. By saying **And if** instead of *but if* he is going beyond what he has just referred to and he is not speaking by way of contrast to what he said. This means that he is not thinking of a teaching regarding Christian maturity which was false, but of something else, indeed anything else to do with the Christian scheme or life. On such matters which, though they have a place, are not as important as those he has been illustrating and enforcing, some differences clearly existed in the church. While no disagreement can be allowed about the former, it may be permitted with regard to the latter.

The second difficulty arises from the fact that Paul seems to guarantee that God will resolve such disagreements and what is more do so by revelation. What about this? Two matters need to be considered.

First we raise the question, What is God said to reveal? The

answer is in the Greek word meaning *this* which the NIV
renders as **that too**, referring to **think differently** and not
different thoughts, that is, different conclusions. The assurance given should not be understood as if it held out the
guarantee that God will see to it that there will be complete
agreement about everything in the church on earth. Instead,
what he promises is that if anyone thinks in a way which is
not in keeping with the outlook or mindset described, God
will reveal to that person *the inappropriateness of his or her
thinking*, provided that person is concerned about the main
things.

Secondly, what is meant by **God will make clear to you**?
On the understanding just outlined there is no need to think
in any other terms than that God will disclose to the person
concerned that the way in which he or she is thinking is not
in keeping with the gospel rule. That can be brought about by
God through all sorts of means or none. It was what Paul
prayed for (1:9-11).

But verse 16 introduces an important qualification. It is an
appeal to the Philippians, and Paul includes himself in it, **to
live up to what we have already attained**. Some needed to
give a (much) higher degree of priority to following Christ,
others to refuse to allow differences within the fellowship to
hinder or give them a pretext for not doing so. All of them,
however, Paul included, needed to keep on keeping on, in
harmony with the gospel rule which they all believed and had
been practising.

This firmly expressed advice is so relevant to the matter
of unity among Christian believers. Divisions are often
traceable to elevating unimportant matters to the primary
place and demoting what is primary, or not having the proper
spirit or mind about it.

In verses 18 and 19, a very different way of life is held up to view. It is in marked contrast not only to what the apostle has said about himself and his colleagues in verses 8-17 but also to what he has urged upon the believers at Philippi. It is definitely not in keeping with that pattern and presents a threat to the church. Many are said to follow it. As Paul had not found it a burden to repeat his warning about the Judaizers in verse 1, so he is not reluctant to speak again about those referred to in these verses, assuming as we do that they are not the same people.

The word translated **pattern** in verse 17 is the word which gives us our noun *type*. It means something or someone who is like something or someone else. The idea of resemblance is embedded in the word. In theology, it functions as a technical term, *typology*, which points to the correspondence between things, events and persons in the two main stages of divine revelation viz. before Christ's coming and after Christ's coming, the preparatory and the final, the predictive and the fulfilled (cf. Romans 5:14; Hebrews 8:5).

Literally, the word means *a mark produced by something*, for example, the print left by a nail (John 20:25) or an image which corresponds to the mould from which it is cast (Acts 7:43); the entire tabernacle (Acts 7:44) resembled heaven (Hebrews 9:23,24); it is also used of examples of conduct (1 Corinthians 10:11; 1 Thessalonians 1:7; 2 Thessalonians 3:9).

A lifestyle corresponds to some model or type. For Paul, his colleagues and the mature at Philippi this was the gospel of Christ (cf.1:27). But there were others, many others, whose outlook and conduct made clear that they were **enemies of the cross of Christ**. Their thoughts, values and aims were diametrically opposed to the thoughts and aims which Christ had in dying on the cross. His cross exhibited self-sacrifice to God for the good of others. Nothing could have been more alien to those for whom self-gratification was the dominant and pervasive concern.

Paul has been emphasising that the mind produces the life. The mind not only produces a life which is ongoing but seals a destiny which is unending. The mind which Paul has been commending leads to heaven (verse 14). In verses 18 and 19, the mind of unregenerate people leads to **destruction** (cf. 1:28 and comment there). He teaches the same connection between mind, life and destiny in Romans 8:5-8.

The author speaks about all this in stark terms. No verbs are used in verse 19. With regard to the life which is to be repudiated, **their god is their stomach** and **their glory is in their shame** indicates a disordered and ruinous life in which the physical and the sensual are enthroned and boasted in (Romans 16:18; 1 Corinthians 6:13). This means that they are worshipped because greed is idolatry (Colossians 3:5). This is the expression of a fleshly mind (Romans 8:6) which is earthbound.

By contrast, Christians belong to heaven. That much is quite clear and generally agreed upon from the opening words of verse 20. But what precisely Paul meant by the word which the NIV translates as **citizenship** - a noun which occurs nowhere else in the New Testament but whose associated verb is found in 1:27 - is a debate which has not yet been resolved. It must mean either the state of being a citizen or the state to which the citizen belongs. Though the difference between them is not great, we prefer the latter because what seems to be to the fore in verses 20 and 21 is not what the citizen is to do but what the government will do for the citizen.

Though verses 20 and 21 constitute a confident, even

jubilant assertion, it would be naive not to think that the author intended to supply a reminder by them and perhaps even a rebuke. The realisation of belonging to the city state of Philippi (see introduction) could well have dulled the reality of belonging to heaven and, if that had not happened, then perhaps the intensity of the expectation which Paul describes might not have been shared by all in the church. The word which he uses to describe this anticipation is similar to the word used in verse 13, which depicts the craning of the neck by an athlete about to finish his course. It consistently refers to the finalisation of salvation (Romans 8:19,23,25; 1 Corinthians 1:7; Galatians 5:5; Hebrews 9:28).

This is brought about by the glorious personal return of Jesus of Nazareth to this world. His full Messianic title, **the Lord Jesus Christ**, coupled with the words **from there**, convey an impression of the august nature of the event which is being described (cf. also 1 Thessalonians 1:10; 4:13-5:4; 2 Thessalonians 1:7-10; 2:8-10).

This is *the day of Christ* referred to in 1:6,10 when God's gracious work in believers will be completed. An integral part of the consummation of salvation is the transformation of the bodies of believers. That is what is referred to in these verses. Salvation is not merely spiritual. It is physical too; it will encompass the body. What does this amount to?

Paul has already made clear that his death would mean his being with Christ and the leaving of his body (1:21-24). It is important to remember that at this point because some writers understand **bodies** to mean the whole person. If that is so, can any change for the better take place for the believer *at death* because it is at the Lord's return that the body is transformed? It is, therefore, better to understand **bodies** in the physical sense. To take that view does not carry with it the idea that the body is a throwaway package. It is a wonderful and essential part of the believer but not the whole. The separation which will take place between person and body at death is only temporary.

Making this identification of what is meant by **bodies** in this verse enables a distinction to be recognised between the two terms Paul uses, **transform** and **be like**. The Greek words so translated recall the description of Christ's incarnation in 2:7,8. They are *schema* and *morphe*. Because of the important difference in meaning between those words (see comments on that passage), verse 21 could have been rendered *refashion our lowly bodies so that they will conform to the body of his glory*. This then means that the change which is being referred to will alter the appearance and the constitution of the physical organism so that it will have the essential features (form) of the body of Christ's glory. As a result it will become a fit body for the redeemed spirit.

Though the adjective **lowly** is a decided improvement on *vile* (KJV), it does not reproduce the original adequately. What Paul wrote was the *body of our humiliation*. This means that what is in view here is not the body as originally created but as affected by the Fall of man into sin. It is bodies subject to weakness, dishonour and decay which are being referred to. The believer is a person who is being increasingly renewed in the likeness of Christ but he or she is in a frail body. Nevertheless, that will not be for ever because not only will the body die, but it will be resurrected and renewed to match the glorified spirit. The entire person will then be redeemed into the likeness of Christ (1 Corinthians 15:42-57).

While it is, therefore, in his capacity as Saviour that believers expect Jesus Christ, he will come with power to subdue everything because he is now Lord. Nothing and no one will be able to hold out against his subjugating activity (2:9-11). He will manifest his power with an irresistible energy. Just as easily as creation came into being, so the consummation will come. This is the guarantee that the glorious change with regard to believers' bodies which has been described, will take place. He will be Lord - and every knee will bow.

9. JOY AND PEACE DISRUPTED AND RESTORED: (4:1-9)

This section contains several exhortations. Some of them are not *explicitly* connected either with what precedes or follows them. That, however, is not the case with the exhortation in verse 1. The words **Therefore** and **that is how** connect very strongly with what has preceded. It is probably due to this fact that the NIV has a paragraph division in the text after this verse. This is intended to override the chapter division, but, of course, neither the chapter end nor the paragraphing was the work of the author.

Already in the letter the Philippians have been exhorted to steadfastness (see 1:27ff.). In that context the exhortation is associated with the maintenance and spread of the gospel of Christ (see also 2:16). In chapter 4 the link is with obtaining the full salvation which that gospel alone provides (see the previous verse). Salvation is, therefore, a common thought in both contexts, first that of unbelievers and then of those who have believed. Taken together, it is clear that a church which does not remain faithful to the gospel is not only hindering the salvation of others but also querying its own.

But the church at Philippi was not like that and hence Paul's gladness with regard to their present condition and his triumphant hope for the future (cf. 2:16; 1 Thessalonians 2:19,20). The **crown** which he refers to is the victor's garland (*stephanos*) and not the sovereign's diadem. That can only belong to the Lord who will strengthen him (1:19ff.), as well as enabling them to withstand both religious and materialistic pressures (3:2;18,19).

Just as an exhortation to steadfastness has been given before, so has a call to unity. In view of these facts it is possible that these concluding exhortations are a kind of summary of all the appeals which Paul has made in 1:27-2:4.

Verses 2 and 3 are obviously connected. Two women are singled out by name and each is appealed to with regard to the need for unity (note the repetition of the verb **plead**). In all probability, the noticeable lack of harmony between them, to put it no higher, was at the root of the unease in the fellowship of the church.

Euodia and Syntyche were good women. They had exerted themselves sacrificially in the cause of the gospel at Philippi, along with Paul. Perhaps they were in the original group of women who met for prayer by the riverside (Acts 16:13). If so, they worked as well as prayed. They were good at both. The verb translated **contended at my side** means *to fight together with*. They were warriors in the gospel cause. But, how sad, they were now hindering the very cause which they had co-operated to promote.

From the way in which Paul deals with them it would seem that they were not guilty of any doctrinal or moral waywardness. They had just fallen out over something, or perhaps over nothing. That kind of thing does happen in churches and it is never easy to expose the suspicions, resolve the misapprehensions and then to have them removed. That is why Paul urges a colleague, a **loyal yokefellow** (*Syzygus* means yokefellow but it can also be a personal name), to help Euodia and Syntyche to adopt the right attitude to each other.

But how? Ultimately, there is only one cure for this. It is **to agree with each other in the Lord**. This is the same expression as in 2:2. The cure is, therefore, the mind of Christ (2:5) which means that each is to think of the other as Christ does. Discord is one of the acts of the sinful nature and it breeds others (Galatians 5:13-26). Behind it is the accuser of the brethren (Revelation 12:10).

The mention of Syzygus leads Paul to think of other colleagues. Clement is a Latin name. Had he been a Roman soldier at one time? If so, he was now in a far better army. The existence of others is acknowledged about whom nothing is known. Their names are not even recorded in the letter. But the all important matter, more important even than to be referred to by name in the Bible, is to have one's name in another book, that is, **the book of life**.

What is this book? It is the register of the people of God (Exodus 32:32, 33) in which the names of the righteous are recorded (Psalm 69:28). They survive the judgement, being chosen and redeemed (Isaiah 4:3; Revelation 3:5;13:8;17:8; 20:15). The Lord Jesus told his disciples to rejoice above all else that their names were written in heaven (Luke 10:20).

Though the exhortation in verse 4 seems to stand alone, it has, like the previous two, been issued already (cf. 2:18,29; 3:1). Paul makes several references to joy and rejoicing in this letter, underlining its importance to the Philippians, but the way in which he speaks in this verse is emphatic. The basic form of the command he issues is **Rejoice in the Lord**. But he declares that this is always to be done, that is, in every experience and circumstance. Then he not only repeats the exhortation but prefaces it with **I will say it again**. He is in earnest about this matter and wants the Philippians to be as well.

To be always rejoicing (2 Corinthians 6:10) does not mean a mindless grin or a thoughtless clap but is the result of calling to mind that the Lord is the Lord everywhere and always, both in the world and in the church, from a night in prison, through death to the dawn of glory (1:12,21; 3:20,21). The church at Philippi was born out of joy amid suffering (Acts 16:25). We should always be able not only to speak but to sing because Jesus is Lord of all.

The exhortation to **gentleness** in verse 5 is the one which seems to be least connected with what precedes it, whether it is viewed in the immediate context or in relation to all that has gone before in the letter. The other question to be faced is why Paul followed it with a declaration about the nearness of the Lord.

We look first at the exhortation to gentleness. It is not easy either to fix the meaning of the Greek word *epieikeia* with precision or to find a single word in the English language which will satisfy everyone. However, the term **gentleness** certainly points in the right direction. It refers to a demeanour, to speech and conduct toward others. It stands opposed to being violent in 1 Timothy 3:3. In James 3:17 it is closely associated with being peace-loving. Clearly, what is in view is considerateness and sensitivity to others even unbelievers (cf. Acts 24:4).

The introduction of this term may be connected with Clement, mentioned in verse 3, whose Latin name means *mild*, or *kind*. Perhaps having become a Christian he lived up to his name for few soldiers would have been naturally mild. But whether that is so or not, meekness and gentleness was certainly seen in Jesus Christ (2 Corinthians 10:1). Here is another link with his mind (2:5). Perhaps it was that realisation which led Paul to go on to speak about the Lord's nearness.

The Lord is near can be understood in relation to space or time. With regard to the former, he is geographically near to his people by his providential activity on their behalf (see 1:12,13,19) and by his Spirit supplying them with gracious aid (1:20). If this is how the expression is to be understood, it means that a believer can look to the Lord to help him or her to be gentle and to bring good out of every situation. If the nearness of the Lord is to be thought of in relation to time, the reference is to *his drawing near*, that is, in glory at the end of time (3:20,21). But perhaps the distinction which we are making would not have entered into the mind of Paul and the early Christians because to them Jesus was near in both senses.

Though the next two verses are linked by no more than a simple conjunction, their relationship can be seen in a more specific way. Verse 6 has often been regarded as introducing a condition for the obtaining of what is promised in verse 7, that is, unless anxiety is successfully dealt with, there is no hope of obtaining peace. While there is something in that, inasmuch as the two cannot coexist in the same person, too much emphasis should not be placed on verse 6 as being conditional because it is not expressed in that form. It is an exhortation to a course of conduct which will yield the consequence described in verse 7. The tone throughout is therefore positive. If the conditional element were to be emphasised, it would wrongly suggest that the blessing was to be merited.

The exhortation in verse 6 is composed of two elements, namely, a prohibition and a positive alternative. We will consider each in turn and then move on to the promised consequent blessedness.

The prohibition, **Do not be anxious about anything**, echoes the teaching of the Lord Jesus Christ in the Sermon on the Mount (Matthew 6:25-34). It is categorical in its tone and total in its scope. Just as joy in the Lord is always appropriate; anxiety never is. The former becomes the gospel; the latter does not because the Lord who is near is in control of everything. Anxiety over needs and difficulties creates an internal distraction which is the antithesis and opponent of peace.

Paul's counsel for dealing with difficulties, **but in everything, by prayer and petition, with thanksgiving, present your requests to God**, is as precisely framed and as complete as the prohibition. It consists of doing something as well as not doing something else at one and the same time. The way to become anxious about nothing is to be prayerful about everything.

Praying includes giving thanks and not only presenting petitions. While these may be expressed to others, they are to be made known to God. Prayer is literally *towards* God. This requires an orientation of *oneself* to him which may be what prayer means in this verse as distinct from petition. Praying takes place in the presence of God. To reel off requests and expect worries to vanish into the thin air is not what is in view here.

The way in which thanksgiving is included in this verse implies the human tendency to forget what one has received when one is acutely aware of present needs. But to do so is not only to forget past benefits (Psalm 103:2) but to ignore the present benefit of having a God who is worthy of the name to pray to. He exists and rewards those who diligently seek him (Hebrews 11:6).

The peace of God is an expression which is only used here in the entire New Testament. It is neither peace with God nor just a peace from God. By faith in him, sinners are at peace with God and he with them. This is reconciliation and it is dealt with in 2 Corinthians 5:18-21.

But the peace *of* God is the peace which *belongs to* God. That is why *peace from God* is not adequate as a rendering. Angels have peace. But the peace Paul refers to is the unruffled serenity and harmony of the Godhead (Hebrews 13:20). It is that peace which becomes *peace from God* in hearts and minds which would otherwise be turbulent and agitated. It is bound to exceed human comprehension both in its nature and effects. Paul uses another superlative at this point.

Irrespective of whether petitions are answered or not this peace will keep calm the minds and hearts of those who seek God in prayer. The idea of a sentry keeping watch for an enemy is present in this verb **guard** (see 2 Corinthians 11:32). Philippi had a Roman garrison in it.

While heart and mind are often used interchangeably in the New Testament, the fact that they are each preceded by the pronoun **your** in this verse makes it far more likely that they are distinguished.

But what does *heart* mean when it is distinguished from *mind*. The peace of God has already been described as being superior to man's understanding *(nous)*, that is, his reasoning faculty. Here mind is a translation of *noemata* which probably means *thoughts*, the product of the *nous*. *Heart* in the New Testament can include the mind and its thoughts as in 1:7 but here the meaning must be different, namely, feelings or emotions. The meaning, therefore, is that the peace of God will reign over the emotions and thoughts of those who draw near to God in true prayer and that this will come about through the merit of Jesus Christ.

Verses 8 and 9 go together. They are to be associated because, literally rendered, verse 8 ends with *those things* and verse 9 begins with *the things*. Both refer to one and the same set of *things*. In verse 8 they are described in terms of themselves; in verse 9, as they were exemplified in the life of the apostle and, of course, in both verses as they were to characterise the Christians at Philippi.

The two verses are climactic in character. This can be seen from a number of factors. First, verse 8 begins with **Finally** (see comment on 3:1 for the significance of this word). Secondly, verse 9 ends with **the God of peace will be with you**, rounding off the thought of verse 7. This link with verse 7 is even clearer in the original of verse 9 where we have an inversion and an emphasis. Instead of the *peace of God* which, as was mentioned, only occurs here in the New Testament we have the *God of the* (i.e. this) *peace*. Thirdly, this is enhanced by the way in which Paul refers to his ministry in verse 9, summarising all that he taught by word of mouth and by way of personal example, and calling on the Philippians to put those things into practice. In the light of this, the strong possibility exists that the content of this exhortation summarises all that has gone before in the letter with regard to the kind of thinking and living which is in keeping with the gospel.

That is our understanding of these verses, but there is another way of regarding them which must be mentioned, though we will not adopt it. Several commentators see the six groups of things listed in verse 8 as being the virtues which were highly regarded and sought after by many in the Graeco-Roman world. But such an identification would have the effect of making Paul appeal to Christians to live as good a life as the best of pagans, whereas the whole of the letter has been to commend what becomes the gospel of Christ and not the good life of the philosophers. We set this aside as lame and an anti-climax.

In support of regarding these things as spiritual realities is the fact that these six terms are used in the Greek Old Testament to translate Hebrew words which describe moral and beneficent aspects of the godly life. Paul could well be doing the kind of thing that the apostle John did when he used the term *logos* to describe Jesus Christ as the word (revelation) of God. *Logos* was a current term of interest and speculation. By its use, John was saying that Jesus Christ was the only ultimate answer to the problems of life and death. By these words, Paul was saying that the only real virtues are those derived from and in keeping with gospel realities.

The structure of verses 8 and 9 is obvious. A series of six objectives is prefaced by the word **whatever** and governed by the verb **think about**. Those things are then to be expressed in action and behaviour as in the case of the apostle Paul. The six groups of things can be regarded as constituting three pairs of similar things viz. the true and noble; the right and pure; and the lovely and admirable.

True and **noble** refer to things from the point of view of their reality. What is true is what is real and what is real, is important. The Hebrew word for *true* is related to the word *Amen* and refers to something sure. The Greek word for *true* relates to what is clear - it cannot be hidden. The word translated *noble* means serious or grave (cf. 1 Timothy 2:2; 3:4,8,11; Titus 2:2,7). The *true* is, therefore, what is sure and clear, namely, gospel certainties and realities, which are second to none in importance.

Right and **pure** refer to things in their moral character and effect. What is *right* is what is in keeping with God's law and what is *pure* is free from any blemish or corruption. These demands and duties are not only pleasing to God but equitable towards others. They are sanctifying to those who do them and act as a restraint on evil in society. They correspond to the effect of salt and light (Matthew 5:13-16).

The next couplet describe things in their appearance to and their effect on others. These terms are not found elsewhere in the New Testament. The first, translated **lovely** (NIV), is made up of two words, namely, *towards* and *love* and refers to that which has a pleasing and agreeable aspect. Such things, for example, gentleness, calmness and joyfulness are all attractive and desirable. The next word, translated **admirable** (NIV), should also be understood in terms of the effect it has but it refers to what is heard rather than to what is seen. *Well sounding* is near its meaning and the kind of testimony described in 2:14 would come into this category.

The final part of verse 8 encapsulates what has been said and enforces it by means of the rhetorical expression **if anything is**. What has been listed is now described as **excellent** and **praiseworthy**. In this connection, the terms which Paul used in his opening prayer need to be recalled. There he refers to the Philippians' need to discern what is best in God's scheme of things and to be filled with fruit of righteousness to the praise of God. That is what is being referred to in these verses. This is the conclusion of the letter and, significantly, it contains a call to use one's mind. Paul pursues the objective for which he has prayed by means of a word from God. The promise that the God of peace and not merely the peace of God will be with them as they ponder and put into effect his instruction is the pinnacle of the letter.

10. GIFTS, GIVING AND THE GIVER: (4:10-20)

Two problems have to be faced with regard to this section. The first relates to its position in the letter. Coming as it does after what seems to be a fitting conclusion with its final note and glorious benediction, it has been thought that originally these verses were part of another letter which Paul wrote to the Philippians. Secondly, its content raises a question. It expresses thanks for further kindness received. Assuming these verses were originally part of this letter, why did Paul delay saying a word of thanks until so late?

On the first score, as has been mentioned in connection with 3:1 (see the note there), the word *finally* does not of necessity mean that the letter is about to be concluded, only that a definite stage in its winding up has been reached. In addition, no extant manuscript evidence exists for this letter minus these verses. Indeed, it is harder to think of an explanation for their being subsequently tacked on than for Paul having included them in the first place.

Proceeding on the basis of their genuineness, the second question has to be answered. Why did Paul wait so long before mentioning and responding to their kindness? To be exact, he had not been silent about it. He had referred to *their partnership in the gospel from the first day until now* (1:5) and to the Philippians that would mean that their gift was being acknowledged in terms of its significance. What is more, Paul wrote that at the very beginning of the letter. Now that he comes to focus on the matter more directly he again refers to the gospel (4:15-16). In addition, he had indicated how much he had appreciated their care by what he said about the messenger they had sent as well as their gift (2:25,30). To Paul and to the Philippians (we suspect) there were more important things than money and more important dimensions

to it than its amount - assuming that it was a monetary gift.
4:10-20 is therefore no belated thankyou note - an afterthought.

Paul writes with a masterly delicateness in these verses,
giving an example of the insight which he prayed the
Philippians would come to possess. He has to strike a balance
between being truly appreciative of their help while making
it clear that he is not wholly dependent on them. That is a
verbal knife edge. The dangers which lie on either side are
either to appear ungrateful or covetous. That is what verses
10-13 are all about.

In the first part of verse 10 he makes it clear that he has
been immensely heartened by their fresh display of concern
for him. The verb that he uses describes the new growth of
springtime. But he immediately adds that he knew of their
desire to assist him even when no gift could be sent through
lack of **opportunity**. Perhaps they did not know where he
was when they had the resources and at other times were in
straitened circumstances themselves (2 Corinthians 8:1,2).
Such statements would assure the Philippians not only that
Paul was grateful but understood what was in their hearts
towards him when they could not actually send him anything.
He **had learned to be content whatever the circumstances**.

Contentment was a much sought after goal in Paul's day,
representing the pinnacle of virtuous attainment. It meant
becoming indifferent to circumstances so as to accept one's
lot impassively. This was achieved by discovering a sufficiency in oneself, an inner strength. Paul uses (in verse 11)
the very word *autarkeia* which was current in his day but fills
it with Christian truth. Such a ploy on his part strengthens the
possibility that he did the same in verses 8 and 9 (see the
comment there).

What, then, did Paul mean by *contentment*? Was the idea

of sufficiency, which is inherent in the word, alien to his thinking? That this was not the case can be seen from his use of the word in 2 Corinthians 9:8 where he writes *in all things and at all times, having all that you need*. The term also appears in the well known statement *Godliness with contentment is great gain* (1 Timothy 6:6). The question is, how did Paul use it in this passage.

First, it does not mean an acceptance of one's lot through becoming indifferent to its circumstances. Twice in verse 12 Paul writes **I know** in order to emphasise that he has actually experienced what is involved both in being in need and in having much more than he needs. The rest of the sentence expands on this in order to underline the point still further.

Clearly, being *content* in a Christian sense does not mean pretending that the circumstances of life do not exist or that they have no effect on the body (hunger) or the mind (need). The same applies to sickness. Not only is the *health and wealth gospel*, (current popular teaching which claims that Christians have a God-given right to be both healthy and rich), disapproved of in principle by this statement but it is also shown that the emphasis of this false teaching is not on contentment irrespective of the circumstances. The question is therefore necessarily raised as to whether such teaching can beget true godliness.

Secondly, Paul's contentment was not only a composure within the circumstances but a rising above them. This was through the strengthening of one who, after all that is said about him in chapter 3, does not even need to be named (verse 13). The statement of verse 13, **I can do everything through him who gives me strength**, is not to be understood as if it meant that Paul was an omnipotent wonder worker. The Christian is not omni-competent. The *everything* in this verse refers back to **any and every situation** in verse 12. By a strengthening supply from without and not the summoning up of resources from within, Paul not only coped with the tyranny of circumstances/experiences, whether favourable or unfavourable, but conquered them. The same could and should be true for the Philippians and for Christian people generally.

Such contentment was of a wholly different kind from that outlook which the sophisticated people of Paul's day sought to obtain. This is Christ-centred and it is sustained by a life which is dependent on him. It becomes the gospel because it is free from complaining (2:14) and glorifies Christ in life and in death (1:20,21).

But it is not easily obtained. Paul uses two verbs which prove this. In verse 11 he writes, **I have learned** and in verse 12, **I have learned the secret of**. Though he found the source and supplier of sufficiency and strength on the Damascus road, namely, God in Christ, it was in the thirty intervening years that he gained contentment.

The first verb (verse 11) means that he was taught in the context of being a disciple and not just a pupil. Living for and with Christ was the classroom situation.

The second verb (verse 12) is taken from the world of the mystery religions - the first century equivalent of the New Age movement - and refers to an initiation process into some secret knowledge. What Paul means by the use of this term is that a heavenly teacher instructed him in what lay beyond the reasoning and reach of the human mind (1 Corinthians 2:6-16) and that he appropriated the lesson in the midst of the ups and downs of life. Through fellowship with Christ in every situation he has become master of the circumstances in which he finds himself.

Though Paul has declared that he was not dependent on the support of the Philippians, he wants them to be sure that their gift was deeply appreciated (verse 14). In describing their action as **good** (*beautiful*) he thinks not merely of its moral quality but its attractiveness. It was a lovely deed (see verse 8). It spoke volumes to him of how they wanted to alleviate those troubles and difficulties which came to him as he served the Lord Jesus Christ. Nor was it the first time that they had done this. Verses 15 and 16 summarise their record in this matter.

In verse 15, Paul writes about what he called *the beginning of the gospel*. The NIV understands this expression as a reference to the initial reception of the gospel by the folk at Philippi and their response to it in cooperation with Paul. That is why it paraphrases at this point with the words **the early days of your acquaintance with the gospel**. That is an acceptable understanding of this pithy expression and it has the advantage over other suggested interpretations of being in keeping with Paul's recollection of the first day in 1:5. What he is emphasising, however, is that the church was concerned about how the gospel was going to be spread almost as soon as they had received it.

When Paul and his colleagues left Macedonia for Thessalonica (cf. Acts 17:1ff.) he did so with an undertaking on the part of the church that it would support him and they honoured that commitment more than once (see verse 16). This was the case when Paul had moved on via Athens to Corinth. In 2 Corinthians 11:8,9 we have an important piece of corroborative evidence on this matter. Also relevant is Acts 18:3,5 which records that, prior to the arrival of Silas and Timothy from Macedonia, Paul was involved in tentmaking. After they came he devoted himself exclusively to preaching. The support of the Philippians which they brought probably freed Paul from the need to divide his time between supporting himself and engaging in the preaching of the word.

Paul proceeds to describe what the Philippians had done in two very different yet complementary ways. In verse 15-18a he borrows language and imagery from the world of financial transactions and in verse 18b from that of sacrificial worship.

He speaks about the matter of **giving and receiving** in verse 15. The familiar Greek word *logos* which is translated **matter** by NIV can mean *account* and the terms for *giving* and *receiving* relate to the two sides of that account, namely, debits and credits. The same word *logos* occurs in verse 17 where the NIV does translate it by the word *account*. In addition, the word *karpos* is found in that verse and while its primary meaning is *fruit* (cf. KJV) it can in certain contexts mean *profit* or *interest*. Finally, the statement **I have received full payment** in verse 18 was often used on receipts issued for monies received.

It looks fairly certain, therefore, that Paul did use banking or commercial terminology. The interesting question is why he did so. To say that it provided an illustration which came readily to mind ignores the fact that Paul endorsed it as suitable for his purpose. Why did he think that? Two emphases which are found in the passage may give clues.

The first is that the Philippians had been business-like in their thinking as to how to support the spread of the gospel. That is the impression given from verse 15. Was this Lydia's influence? She was a business woman and it was in her house that the church first met (Acts 16:14,40). It is not impossible or inappropriate for a church to be business-like and spiritually minded. Secondly, Paul wants to stress that giving is not losing or giving away. It is not a writing off but an investing in the bank of heaven. A return will be forthcoming and it will be at compound rate. It will abound. God rewards his people in excess of what they expend (2 Corinthians 9:8-11).

In the course of using the commercial language Paul has spoken of spiritual principles. He has indicated the effect of their gifts on him in qualitative as well as quantitative terms. He has been filled and his needs have been more than met (verse 18).

In the second analogy, he brings out the Godward dimension of such giving and makes clear that God was delighted with it. The gifts which Epaphroditus brought to Paul were in the nature of sacrificial offerings from the church to God. Paul saw that and he therefore rejoiced in the Lord as he received them (cf. verse 10; also 1 Chronicles 11:15-19). Though he uses a threefold description about them, the point he makes is one and the same, namely, their acceptableness in God's sight. *Fragrance* represents the reaction of God to acceptable sacrifices (cf. Genesis 8:21; Exodus 29:18). The terms which are used here are reminiscent of those found in Ephesians 5:2 with reference to the death of Christ.

Associated with these words is the twofold fact that, as a consequence of the coming and death of Jesus Christ, worship and priesthood have undergone a transformation. The ritual feature has been removed and access to God is open and free for all believers. Monetary gifts for the support of servants of Christ are fragrant sacrifices and anyone can offer them (Hebrews 13:15-16). Worship is now in spirit and truth and not tied to consecrated places and cultic practices.

In verse 19 Paul is assuring the Christians at Philippi of two glorious certainties. First, the God who had been mindful of his needs would not be forgetful of them in theirs.

Secondly, the supplies which he had received had in no way
diminished the resources which God possessed. Being able to
give a guarantee of such abundant provision leads him into
a doxology.

Paul refers to *every need* in this verse and not **all your
needs** (NIV). While both renderings teach the same truth
with the same certainty, the singular highlights the attentiveness of God towards his people. Not one need will be
overlooked. While the preceding verses have been concen-
trating on material need, it would be very strange to think that
Paul intended to exclude spiritual needs from the scope of this
promise, particularly as the physical needs he refers to were
connected with the service of the Lord. The promise is
therefore to be linked with all the needs of the Philippians
which have been prayed for and spoken about in the letter,
individual and relational, in the church and in the world.

Provision for every need does not only require an infinite
knowledge but also resources of equal magnitude. These are
pointed up in the words **according to his glorious riches in
Christ Jesus**. We prefer a word for word rendering of the
Greek, *according to his riches in glory in Christ Jesus*. This
statement can be considered in three steps.

First, *according to his riches*. The riches of God are a
theme which Paul had emphasised in the letters to the
Ephesians and Colossians which he had just written (Ephesians 1:7,18; Colossians 1:27; 2:2), but what is in view here
is not so much his wealth but his bounty. God will supply not
merely *out* of his riches but *according* to them. He is not
niggardly. He does not need to conserve or eke out his
resources. He is generous - incredibly so.

The next step is, *in glory*. These words have been understood to mean *in heaven*. However, to understand them in that

way is to leave the needs of the Philippians in this life unprovided for which is the main point of Paul's testimony. An alternative is to see them as meaning *from heaven*, regarding *in glory* as having adverbial force and describing further God's glorious supply rather than the riches themselves. That is our preference. The other way is to construe them as an adjective and see them as describing the riches. That is the way in which the NIV understands them. Taking them in that way has the advantage, at least, of referring to something which is distinct from the supplying activity. So far, then, we have a declaration that God will generously supply glorious riches to needy Christians.

The final step is, *in Christ Jesus*. This relates to the supplies as well as to the supplying activity and indicates that all this will come about through the merit and mediation of Jesus Christ. *From the fullness of his grace we have all received one blessing after another* (John 1:16).

It is not surprising that praise follows such a promise. The spiritual logic, of course, is that if the Philippians are to be thanked for their gifts, then surely God is to be thanked for all that he gives in and through Jesus Christ. There are three parts to this doxology. The first specifies who is being praised; the second what is being ascribed to him; and the third the length of time during which that praise is appropriate.

It is **God**, the **Father** of his regenerated and adopted children, who is being adored. His fatherhood is specified because of the goodness and kindness which are implicit in the blessing announced. But in spite of his unfailing paternal attentiveness it is his deity which is mentioned first and accentuated. He is God our Father and not our father-God.

Glory is what is ascribed to him. While the glory of God is his self-revelation in whatever way he chooses to make himself known, it is seen supremely in grace in Jesus Christ for the salvation of human beings. To give glory to him is to acknowledge him with the whole being for who he is and what he has done. It is to give him what is due to his holy name (Psalm 29:2). Christians realise that this offering of glory has an eternal dimension.

A resounding **Amen** attests Paul's wholehearted response. The word comes from a Hebrew term which means *to be sure.* Paul has no doubts that God deserves all that is his due and that he will receive it. What is more he wants God to have it for ever.

CLOSING GREETINGS (4:21-23)

If Paul had dictated this letter to an amanuensis, these final words could have been written in his own hand in order to authenticate the whole letter. He did that sometimes, while on other occasions he merely signed his name (cf. 1 Corinthians 16:21; Galatians 6:11; Colossians 4:18; 2 Thessalonians 3:17 and Philemon 19). Forgeries were being circulated (cf. 2 Thessalonians 2:2) and apostolic authority was important.

Paul observed literary convention with regard to the form of the conclusion of this letter just as he did with its commencement; but as he devised his own Christian greeting so he composed a Christian farewell. What he wrote seems to be genuinely informative and nothing more but, in a most disarming way, he is pursuing the main thrust of his letter, emphasising the importance of Christian unity and the sure availability of the gracious disposition and aid of the Lord Jesus Christ. This is his parting shot.

He addresses himself to *every saint in Christ Jesus.* The use of the singular is deliberate because he has been addressing himself to every one in his exhortations. Now by such a personal greeting, he reminds every one that the letter's contents were addressed to him or her individually. No one is mentioned by name so that no one might feel left out. Each is given the dignified status of being a saint (see comment on 1:1). The word **greet** is in the plural so that probably the elders and the deacons were being asked to make sure that such greetings were conveyed to all.

The brothers referred to in verse 21 would have included Timothy and perhaps Luke who was with Paul at Rome (Acts 27:1) while **the saints** are the Christians who were in the vicinity where he was imprisoned. These would have been unknown to the Philippians, but it is important for them to feel that they belong to all who call on the name of the Lord Jesus (1 Corinthians 1:2) and all who love him with an undying love (Ephesians 6:24).

The closing benediction resumes the note in the opening greeting. **Grace** will be **with your spirit**. While *your* is plural, *spirit* is singular. That combination is best understood as a reference to the spirit of each person who makes up the company of the church. The *spirit* is a way of describing the whole person in his or her capacity towards God. God will deal graciously with each of those who turn to him and make such Christians gracious to each other. **Amen** - may it be so - says Paul and hopefully so did each saint in Philippi when the letter was read in the church.

Dr. Hywel Rees Jones graduated with a BA in Hebrew and Old Testament from the University of Wales before studying at Cambridge where he gained a MA in Theology. He taught for a short time at the Bible Training Institute, Glasgow before serving in pastorates at Grove Chapel, London, and Borras Park, Wrexham. He joined the staff of the London Theological Seminary in 1977, becoming the Principal in 1985. He is associate editor of *Foundations*, the theological journal of the British Evangelical Council, and chairman of its Theological Study Conferences. He has published *Gospel and Church* (Evangelical Press of Wales) and edited the addresses given by Martyn Lloyd-Jones at the BEC conferences, published as *Unity In Truth* (Evangelical Press). He is married, with three children and two grandchildren.